OUT OF THE
HOLOCAUST

OUT OF THE
HOLOCAUST

Peter Volodja Boe

ELM HILL

A Division of
HarperCollins Christian Publishing

www.elmhillbooks.com

Out of the Holocaust

Published in Nashville, Tennessee, by Elm Hill, an imprint of Thomas Nelson. Elm Hill and Thomas Nelson are registered trademarks of HarperCollins Christian Publishing, Inc.

Elm Hill titles may be purchased in bulk for educational, business, fund-raising, or sales promotional use. For information, please e-mail SpecialMarkets@ ThomasNelson.com.

All Scripture quotations, unless otherwise indicated, are taken from the New King James Version. © 1982 by Thomas Nelson. Used by permission. All rights reserved.

Library of Congress Cataloging-in-Publication Data

Library of Congress Control Number: 2018953407

ISBN 978-1-595559005 (Paperback)
ISBN 978-1-595559043 (Hardbound)
ISBN 978-1-595559104 (eBook)

World War II Refugee

"For in Him we live and move and have our being".

(ACTS 17:28, NKJV)

DEDICATION

To my wife, Betty

To our four children and their spouses—Nathan and Ruth, Sarah, Justin and Michelle, and Steven and Dana

To our twelve grandchildren—Ethan, Annabelle, David, Claire, Peter, Jeremiah, Gabriella, Brayden, Isabella, Leighann, Landon, and Lawson

To the family members of my late brother, Tom—his wife, Roxanna, and their children—Lisa and Tom Bensen (and their children: Andrew, Joshua, and Katelin); Chris and Mia Boe (and their children: Nicholas and Maria); Daniel and Brenda Boe (and their children: Tommy, twins Charlie and Max, and Brisbin); Benjamin; and Valerie and Jerad Huepenbecker (and their children: Kade, William, and Eli)

To my adoptive parents, Victor and Hilda Boe

To the caregivers at the Baldone Children's Home in the southeastern part of Latvia

To Rose Briede Austrums, who came to the States in the 1950s and married our teacher, Bernards Austrums; Rose was the primary spokesperson on our behalf, and she kept in touch with some of the children through the years.

To the four other women who heroically accompanied us from Latvia to Germany and saw to it that we were fed, clothed, properly sheltered against the elements, and protected from disease, harm, and danger. They always found a way for us, even though there were no guaranteed sources of food, water, or medicine. These four women were Janīna Kurmītis, Alma Mežaks, Smaida Ašenieks, and Alma Rāva.

To Jānis Mežaks, one of our teachers in Germany, and a longtime resident of Canada who now lives in Latvia

To my fellow brethren—missionaries from Denmark and the USA—among whom I served in Nigeria and West Africa, including my former students (1965–1971)

To Lloyd Hildebrand, editorial consultant; his literary, editorial, and publication skills have been an invaluable asset in the compilation and publication of this book.

To so many others who played crucial roles in my development after I was severed from my biological parents in southeastern Latvia, bordering on Belarus

To Kathleen Yeats, a young British woman who paid several visits to our Rohlsdorf home as a Sunday school teacher; she was the first person who introduced Jesus to us through pictures, songs, and her godly example.

CONTENTS

Contents

PREFACE

Throughout the eighty years of my life God has been truly good to me. He has blessed me beyond measure, and I thank Him for everything He has done for me, within me, and through me. Without Him, I can do nothing, but through Him I can do all things. (See John 15:5 and Philippians 4:13.)

This book represents a portion of what I've learned during my eight decades of life, which likely began in Belarus or nearby Latvia. My brother, Thomas Christopher (aka Tolja Sinegins), and I (aka Volodja Sinegins) were considered to be orphans. My mother, who was dying, had surrendered us because she could no longer take care of us.

We were first placed in the Baldone Children's Home, which was located about twenty-one miles southeast of the capital city of Latvia, Riga. Later in 1944, we were taken to Germany and I remember very vividly the fears we experienced as we heard bombs exploding and saw troops marching nearby. The horrors of the war were very real to us.

Faithful people took care of us and protected us as we traveled from Latvia to Germany. It was a very frightening time for us—a time when we knew very little about the world around us and the terrible things that were happening in Europe and elsewhere.

The severance from my biological ties opened the door for me to be assimilated into the larger, extended family of humankind, and it prompted me to search for my true identity. I believe we are all searching for our origins, and that is especially true when we no longer have a record of our biological roots, which was the case with me and my brother. The name and location of our birthplace, as well as the why, how, and when concerning the same, are all unknown due to the loss or destruction of those records during World War II.

Hence, my search for my personal identity began, and it culminated many years later in Jesus Christ, who is the way, the truth, and the life. (See John 14:6.) No one can come to the Father except by Him.

Thanks to the help of Rose Austrums and four other service workers, Tom and I, along with 128 other children, were well cared for while we remained in Germany (throughout the Holocaust) until 1950, when my brother and I were adopted by an American couple, Pastor Victor C. Boe and his wife, Hilda Groberg Boe.

Now you know a little bit about me and my identity. In all likelihood, I have a Belarussian Jewish background. (This is based on a study of my DNA that was done in 2007.) I am a Lutheran pastor, a husband, a father, a grandfather, a writer, and a teacher. For some years (1965–1971) I served as a missionary in Nigeria, West Africa—mostly in the Numan community. But the most important part of my identity is the knowledge that I am a Christian who is rooted and grounded in Christ and His way.

God has created us in His image. We are fearfully and wonderfully made. He is in the process of conforming us into the very image of Christ. This is our destiny as Christians, and what an exciting destiny it is.

Christ within us is the hope of glory, and He enables us to know who we are in Him. There is such a vast difference between believing in Him and actually knowing Him, as the following Scripture reveals:

"and be found in Him, not having my own righteousness, which is from the law, but that which is through faith in Christ, the righteousness which is from God by faith; that I may know Him and the power of his resurrection...".

(PHILIPPIANS 3:9–10, NKJV)

It is wonderful for me to be able to say that I know Him, and the power of His resurrection can be seen throughout this book.

INTRODUCTION

Before I formed you in the womb I knew you;
Before you were born I sanctified you;
I ordained you a prophet to the nations.
(JEREMIAH 1:5, NKJV)

Early Memories

One of my earliest memories came about when we were living with our mother (Miss Sinegins) in a small apartment in a two-story home that was located either in Belarus or lower Latvia. I remember my brother Tolja (aka Tom) yelling, "You cut me with the scissors!"

I replied, "No, I did not."

"Yes, you did, Volodja!" (Volodja was my real name, and it is an affectionate term that stems from the Russian name Vladimir.)

Our mother intervened, and everything went back to normal.

I feel quite certain that Tom and I—Tolja and Volodja Sinegins—are blood brothers. *Mūs esam brāļi!* (We are brothers!) We were always together in those early days. I recall that our home was sparsely furnished. Even so, it was home to me and I always felt safe there.

One day, while playing outside, I needed to go to the toilet. I remember a man taking me to an outhouse nearby and lifting me above an open hole so I could "go potty." This was new to me because we had always used a chamber pot inside our home. I remember that large hole so clearly and the horrible smells that emanated from it, and I was frightened. I wondered what would happen if I slipped from the man's hands and fell into that stinking hole. I clung to the man very tightly even though he attempted to assure me that there was nothing to worry about.

My mother had a spinning wheel that she used for spinning a bundle of thread onto a spool that she used for knitting. I recall a time when the back door was open and my mother was hanging clothes on a line outside. There was fresh, bright snow on the ground. I could not remember having seen snow before, and my mother coaxed me to come outdoors with her. As I did so, I found myself in waist-deep snow!

A couple of times she took Tolja and me to a Finnish steam house where we sat naked on boards and inhaled the hot, steamy air. This was supposed to be good for us, but after we returned home with fleas jumping all over our bodies, we never went there again!

In one of the rooms on the first floor of the house in which we lived, there was a mother with two daughters. We never really got to know them but would see them from time to time. Some elderly invalids, who may have been victims of the war, lived upstairs. I remember being quite frightened once when one of them reached out to touch me and greet me. However, when that man gave me some candy my fears diminished.

Winters were rough in that area. Often, the snow was hip deep! During the spring and summer months, though, my mother would take us for walks, and we would sometimes visit our neighbors. In one of the homes we visited, a little boy showed us his toys, including strings of empty thread spools. How I wished I could have such chains of spools and other toys.

On other occasions we would walk through the nearby rolling hills that were resplendent with beautiful flowers, including daisies, which were used by beautifully dressed young ladies as crowns during the local fall festival.

Most of the memories I'm sharing here relate to the years when I was four or five years old. I have no memories of events in my life prior to that time.

As to the fate or identity of my father, very little is known. At most I saw him only a couple of times. I remember him to be a short man of light weight with a joyful mood. I remember he once gave me a horseback ride and I recall sitting on his lap. At the time I believed he was my biological father. It is likely that he became a Belarussian-partisan fighter aligned with the Russians against the Germans. The Germans, as you may know, were bent on exterminating all "inferior" and undesirable people, and this, from their point of view, included many Belarussians and Latvians.

The Nazis victimized millions of people in death camps and gas chambers. These victims included Jews, Jehovah's Witnesses, homosexuals, Gypsies, Roman Catholics, mentally and physically challenged people, those who they branded as "social misfits," and anyone who aided Jews. These were challenging times.

Throughout this book I will be sharing personal stories, along with scriptural teaching. I have so much to share, and I feel particularly fortunate to be able to do so in this book. It is my desire to show you how I came to know the way of eternal oneness and fellowship in Jesus Christ. This gave me a sense of being a member of God's family even though I was cut off from my biological family and roots during World War II.

Talents and Gifts

My studies have included various languages, human nature, theology, psychology, anthropology, and many other subjects. I have formally studied the following languages: English (one of my college majors), Latvian, German, Latin, Greek, Aramaic, Hebrew, and Hausa, though I must admit that my fluency in languages other than English is not as good as it once was.

Some who are not always thinking in religious terms are guided by God's will in the application of their specific skills, talents, and special gifts. Some may have musical, artistic, medical, agricultural, mathematical, scientific, linguistic, writing, intuitive, and many other specialized talents and gifts at which they excel and which they apply in God's service without, say, quoting Scripture at every point. For example, a surgeon can still be divinely guided without focusing his or her attention on the Lord or Scripture-based logic. The application of your special gifts and talents is much appreciated, especially when directed toward the improvement of our lives, health, and well-being.

The same could be said of inventors and other professionals who are guided by a creative impulse that stems from the Creator himself. Each person seems to possess specific talents that are like gifts in their lives. Some may have musical talents, while others do well with writing, teaching, science, business, and mathematics. Whatever your talent, it can be used for creative purposes that can help others in a variety of ways.

No matter what our talents and gifts may be, we should never feel superior (or inferior) to others. We are all equally important in the grand scheme of things. We complement and even complete one another as we apply our various gifts and talents.

We have been called to preach and proclaim the Word of God through our words, actions, and appropriate behaviors. Empowered by the Spirit of Christ, we are able to emit, reveal, and speak the truth to others. In so doing we become living commentaries and walking illustrations of God and His Word. This is so important for us to realize.

St. Paul wrote, "You are our epistle written in our hearts, known and read by all men; clearly you are an epistle of Christ, ministered by us, written not with ink but by the Spirit of the living God, not on tablets of stone but on tablets of flesh, that is, of the heart."

(2 CORINTHIANS 3:2–3, NKJV)

What are people reading when they see and hear you? Does your witness draw them closer to Christ? Does it improve their lives?

Spiritual Discernment

According to the ladies who helped us (Rose Austrums, in particular), my brother and I were the only two undocumented children in the entire group of 130 who were taken to Germany. However, the lack of documentation and my inability to know my birth date do not really cause me any concern, because I now know I am a member of the family of God in Jesus Christ, and this is a sufficient-enough cause for me to live a lifetime of eternal joy.

True spiritual discernment comes to those who can continually differentiate between the way of Christ and the way of human nature. This comes about when we seek Him with all our hearts, minds, souls, and strength.

Remember this, being religious will save no one. Jesus does the saving in His timing and according to His purposes. Wait upon Him and He will lead you.

The Lord Jesus Christ gives us certainty even during extremely uncertain times and challenging circumstances.

Whenever possible, I document and support my statements with truth from the Holy Scriptures, a personal knowledge of Jesus Christ, and my understanding of human nature.

Peter Boe

CHAPTER 1

DARK DAYS OF INSECURITY
AND FEAR

There is neither Jew nor Greek, there is neither slave nor free,
there is neither male nor female; for you are all one in Christ Jesus.
And if you are Christ's, then you are Abraham's seed,
and heirs according to the promise.
(GALATIANS 3:28–29, NKJV)

The profound truths that we are all one in Christ Jesus and that we are Abraham's seed became very real to me as I got older. The promise that Paul was referring to here is this: If we belong to Christ Jesus (are in Him who is Abraham's seed), then we are Abraham's offspring and his spiritual heirs. This is what permits us to be members of God's family, His adopted children.

The Nazi Occupation of Latvia

Nazi Germany completed its occupation of Latvia on July 10, 1941. Latvia became a part of Germany's *Reichskommissariat Ostland*—the Province General of Latvia. Those who were not racially acceptable to the Nazis or those who opposed the German occupation, along with those who had cooperated with the Soviet Union, were killed or were sent to concentration camps.

The Germans of this time were particularly focused on eliminating Jews and Gypsies. Thirty thousand Latvian Jews were shot in the autumn of 1941. The remaining population of Jews were rounded up and put into ghettos. In November and December 1941, the Rīga Ghetto became very crowded and to make room for the imminent arrival of German Jews, 30,000 Jews in Rīga were taken from the ghetto to the nearby Rumbula Forest where they were shot to death.

During the years of Nazi occupation, 90,000 people in Latvia were killed. Approximately 70,000 of these were Jews and 2,000 were Gypsies. The remainder consisted of people from various backgrounds. Resistance in Latvia was very confusing during this time, because it included people who were resisting Soviets on the one hand and Germans on the other. In addition, Soviet supporters were resisting the German occupation. The nationalists resisted everyone who tried to occupy Latvia.

Many people within the resistance movements ended up joining the German or Russian armies. Very few were able to live as independent bands in the forests. Some Latvians resisted the German occupation with great bravery. One of these was Zanis Lipke, who risked his life to save more than fifty Jews.

During World War II more than 200,000 Latvians ended up in the rank and file of both occupation forces (German and Russian), and approximately half of them were killed on the battlefield. This was what life was like in my homeland of Latvia during the Holocaust.

So, as you can see, Eastern Europe and Germany were enshrouded by dark clouds of fear and uncertainty when Tolja and I were very little boys. One night, for example, we heard that many people, mostly Jews, were being rounded up and massacred by the soldiers we could see walking in the distance between wooded areas. (During this time Russians were deporting various leaders and others to Siberia, as well.) My mother took us to a barn, which became our hiding place that night, and several other people were there with us.

One day, not long afterward, my brother and I saw a procession of people following a horse-pulled hearse. Most of the people were wearing black as they marched toward a cemetery. We wondered what was happening, because we did not understand anything about death or dying. Not long thereafter, however, our mother took us to the funeral of a young girl.

We watched with rapt attention as the casket was lowered into a freshly dug grave by four men holding two long straps. After the casket was lowered, dirt was shoveled on top of it. The girl's mother wailed and cried very loudly, and everyone, including us, was gripped by sadness and even some fear. At one point it seemed as if the girl's mother would fall into the grave on top of the casket because she was leaning precariously over the open grave. I wondered if she wanted to join her daughter in the burial.

During the springtime, the cemetery became a place where my brother and I would run and play while our mother would sit on a bench in the sunshine and listen to the birds singing. It was a very serene and idyllic setting. There was something very special about the peace I experienced in that natural setting.

We did not worship in any particular church or synagogue, though Tolja said that he had faint recollections of us going to a church when we were quite small. Whatever the case, I developed a God-consciousness that grew out of my deep respect for the word *Dievs*, which means God in Latvian.

Major events were soon to transpire at our home and the sense of peace we had experienced began to dissolve. Our mother became sick and called for a doctor. I remember that he used a two-piece, wooden stethoscope to listen for her heartbeat. Not long afterward our mother told us, "I am dying." We had absolutely no idea of how to respond to this dreadful announcement that she had shared very matter-of-factly with us.

Our mother struggled to provide for the family. There was hardly any food in our home, except for soup bones and broth along with some bread. We would chew the beef off the bones for several days until the bones were completely white. We were literally starving and had no idea what might happen next. Lack of proper sanitation and access to nutritious and adequate food in the war environment contributed to our destitute situation.

Our mother told us that we would be going "someplace" before long. In one way this was exciting news to us, but we did not really know what she had in mind. We began to wonder where we would be going and how we would get there.

Before long our mother took us to a local tailor to have us measured for clothing. A few days later we were neatly dressed in brand-new jackets and pants, which were most likely made from army blankets. We were given new mittens, and our mother put some paper money into our coat pockets. She then took us outside to wait, but we did not know what we were waiting for.

After a while, a greenish-gray bus that had bullet holes in its side appeared. Our mother took us to the bus, hugged us tightly, and helped us to get in. We thought we would all be going on a long journey together. It was only then that we realized she would not be accompanying us. Both Tolja and I began to scream and cry as the doors of the bus closed. It was a terribly frightening time. As the bus pulled off, we lost sight of our mother. It was the last time we ever saw her! Other passengers tried to comfort us. They gave us candy and eventually we fell asleep.

When we awoke, we found ourselves wrapped in blankets and riding in a horse-drawn carriage. Some adults were with us. The carriage took us to the state-run Baldone Children's Home in Latvia. It became our new home, at least for a while. Tolja and I grew very close to each other during this time, inasmuch as we were all the family we both now had. Adapting to a new home environment was not easy. We cried our hearts out, yes, but after we lived through the initial shock and arrived at the Baldone Home, we began to adapt quickly to the new environment. We came to regard the other children as part of an extended family, along with numerous, caregiving parental figures and aides.

Parting with us was no doubt a hurtful experience for our mother. We did not comprehend her grief. We were more concerned about our own destiny. The sense of closeness I lost with my parents, I eventually regained through adoption and marriage.

Both my brother and I had become totally dependent on our parents for all our basic survival needs, much like infants still in the womb, and we were frightened by being suddenly severed from this line of support. We, like most infants and children, had an attitude of entitlement. Within the resultant crying and screaming is an element of anger, resentment, fright, and panic.

Without tender, loving care infants can wilt away and even die. But our experience showed us that such care can be provided by nonbiological caregivers. When children are torn away from natural ties, other adults can enter the picture as surrogates. As it turned out, we were much better provided for throughout our journey than are many babies and children in abusive households. Some are abandoned, aborted, or left to die.

For those who took care of us, we are most grateful and for all the human "angels" who materialized along the way. We learned early on the difference between nuclear and extended family bonding. The latter is much more common in parts of the world where the population is ravaged and decimated by disease, warfare, and tragedy. The nuclear family, as we know it, is foreign concept for many around the globe! We adapted, and we survived!

A New Home

I was glad that Tolja and I were at the new location together. He was at least one familiar face among so many totally strange, unfamiliar faces. I did not bond closely and intimately with the other children, but such close bonding is frequently not present even in nuclear families.

At times we felt insecure and intimidated by the new people, new surroundings, and our new home. We moved into a large two-story brick building (the Baldone Children's Home) where a very kind, middle-aged lady greeted me and led me to a wooden bench. As I sat there, I noticed a little girl who had pus-filled sores all over her body. She seemed very depressed and alone. It seemed as if no one wanted to get near her. Even so, she never complained, but I noticed her weeping from time to time.

The lady who greeted me had a son who was only a few years older than me. He was a very friendly boy who had a knack for telling fantastic stories, most of which I believed with some reservations. I noticed that he had a rubber tube that was attached to his body. He kept it curled under his shirt. I assumed that this was to help him with his digestive system in some way or another.

Anytime any of us developed an infection, even a slight one, the nurse would take us to a small, medicine-filled room. We would have to take off all our clothes so she could examine us and smear salve on the infected places on our skin.

Sometimes we were able to play freely with one another, but I usually kept to myself. Once, when the subject of God came up, some of the boys engaged in mockery. It was very disrespectful. They would lower their trousers and put their buttocks near the window and say, "See! That's what we think of God!" And then they would laugh. I found this to be very disturbing even though my knowledge of God was extremely limited at the time.

Nonetheless, my God-consciousness began to develop at this early stage, and I detested it greatly when anyone would mock Him. I began to wonder how I could learn more about Him.

Much of our time was spent outdoors, mostly in the nearby playground. We would play in the sand pit, and many of the children believed that if we pounded sticks into the sand it would rain. I thought this was an interesting theory, so I decided to try it out on a sunny but partly cloudy day. Guess what? It rained! However, I did not like rainy weather very much at all, so I decided I wouldn't try that again!

The caretaker (handyman) was always very nice to us. He took care of the horses and chickens, and would sometimes let the older boys take the horses and their wagons into town. I noticed that he had lost some of his fingers. I asked him how this happened and he explained that he lost his fingers due to an accident with a saw.

He showed us how to comb and part our hair. He said that parting our hair on the left side was the correct way, and that's the way I've parted my hair ever since.

A funeral procession caught my attention one afternoon. A long line of somber persons walked before and after the casket, which was covered with a wreath and beautiful flowers. They were singing a dirge in slow rhythm as they approached the Baldone Children's Home in which the funeral was held. One man played a violin. It became my impression that this funeral was for the little girl with open sores that I had observed soon after I arrived in my new home.

They served split-pea soup to all of us who attended the funeral. I remember that most of the food that was served in the home was excellent. It was certainly far better than anything I'd eaten before.

Signs of War

In the early spring of 1944, the signs of war appeared dramatically in our area. Several tanks could be seen among the trees to the west of our building, and lines of soldiers in military vehicles with guns attached to them were moving along the road to the east of our building. Even while we were picking blueberries nearby we would encounter groups of soldiers who were resting on the ground.

It was explained to me that these soldiers were Germans—our "friends" who would liberate us from Russian captivity. It was all very scary, as these soldiers began to occupy our home. They set up their rifles on tripods on the yard in front of the building and pointed them at moving targets, usually model airplanes that were pulled along on horizontal wires. Thank God those rifles were never live-fired or pointed at us. Just hearing the gunfire was scary enough, though. Sometimes the soldiers would eat honey from buckets and when they were finished, they would throw the buckets in our direction. I can still remember the delicious taste of that honey, which we lapped up as a delicious treat.

However, we were soon forced out of our rooms on the upper floors, and we were compelled to sleep in the tunnel that we approached through the kitchen. Soon thereafter we were on the move, inasmuch as the situation in the home had become very critical for the children, and our helpers and our counselors knew we could no longer stay there. We had stayed at the Baldone home for about a year.

Then we began to walk to Rīga. Most of us walked the entire way, approximately twenty miles, but some rode atop the horse-drawn or oxen-pulled, fully loaded wagons. As we headed out on a gravel road, we all paused at a small shed by the road where we watched the ladies make strawberry jam sandwiches. On top of our empty stomachs, they were delicious!

We heard what seemed to be a distinct humming sound when we put our ears next to some utility poles. These sounds likely came from the transformers. Closer to Rīga we saw dead horses and cattle along the roadway. It was a scary sight for us to behold, partly because we were uncertain as to whether or not the animals were actually dead. We wondered if they might still be alive and would be capable of jumping up and lunging at us. We saw one farmer frantically attempting to round up his cows, which had been scattered by strafing and bombing planes. Unfortunately, most of his herd had apparently been killed!

Whenever we would hear the approaching sound of warplanes, we would jump into the woods, but much of our journey was relatively quiet. While walking through the wooded area, I found a small, thin, black plastic canister with a creamy white substance within it. I licked it, not realizing it may have been highly toxic or even lethal. Fortunately, we did not set off unexploded hidden bombs that were often found on active battlefields. We stopped for rest, snacks, water, and body relief all along the way. Eventually we reached the city of Rīga, Latvia.

Many of the buildings there had been bombed out and were reduced to piles of rubble. We sometimes entered these partially standing buildings. We attempted to board a streetcar, and we pulled on an inner ceiling cable to make it go, but no luck. The electric power cables had been blown apart. Some German officers were directing traffic by using metal-handled discs, but the traffic seemed hopelessly bottled up!

In one of the partially damaged buildings we were served freshly cooked carrots in bowls, but a bomb exploded close to us and shattered glass got into our food, rendering it inedible. In the same building or in one very much like it, we spent the night sleeping in the basement on a layer of straw that was atop a dirt floor. Mice scurried all around us! Most of the buildings were badly damaged already. We did not notice much additional bombing and strafing in that particular location.

We were placed on a long, flat-bed trailer and taken to the Majori Children's Home in the Jūrmala suburb of Rīga. It was about fifteen miles away, near the Baltic Sea. We were positioned as our names were called off. One teenaged girl wanted desperately to go with us, but when she was not accepted, she cried out in utter frustration and threw down a packet of photos and possibly even her ID documents. No doubt there were quite a few children and teens who had been orphaned by the war and were begging for survival provisions, protection, and caring homes. (When we visited Rīga many years later, in the late 1990s and early 2000s, we observed many beggars on the streets, and some were very young. This reminded me of the children begging many years ago.)

Majori Children's Home

When we arrived at the Majori Children's Home in the Jūrmala suburb of Latvia's capital city of Rīga, we were quartered in a couple of small, shed-like buildings. All available rooms in the main, thatch-roofed, multi-storied building were already occupied by other children. We stayed there for about two weeks, but this is where we met Rose/Rozīte Austrums. I also got to know Smaida Ašenieks, the head nurse, who eventually moved to Canada. They read off the list of our names and confirmed that we were supposed to be there, and they warmly welcomed us.

In one of the larger rooms upstairs the children were routinely "bathed" by large heat lamps that were suspended from the ceiling. We would lie naked on our backs, wearing only dark-lensed glasses. This is still practiced with children in the northern countries of Europe, where there is less sunlight per year and vitamin D deficiency is feared. When we moved to Germany, attempts were made to take these large, rectangular lamps along with us, but they eventually had to be abandoned along the way.

A whole new era in my life was about to begin. My brother and I were assigned to a room that had enough bunk beds for six to eight children. We soon became friends with the others, and would often converse with one another until we fell asleep.

We were served a great variety of foods at the home. Some of those foods were split-pea soup, baked apples, thick cake pretzels (which were served on St. John's Day—a day when we honored everyone named John), delicious creamy cereals (with cinnamon and sugar on top), slices of bread with butter, and some ham. We also enjoyed cringles, handmade pastries from Danish dough. We were weighed regularly on a heavy platform scale.

One day, the Majori head nurse—Smaida Ašenieks—through an open window, heard a young boy's sweet voice singing beautifully and loudly, "*Kur tu teci, kur tu teci, Gailīti man?*" This is translated as "Where are you running, where are you running, rooster, my dear?" When she looked out, she saw that it was Tolja! He had a good voice, which he utilized throughout the years by singing in high school and college choirs, and singing solos for special occasions. He also played the French horn in his high school band.

I remember Smaida also as the nurse who called me several times into her medical treatment room to attempt to clean my left ear with a metal syringe and pump. This cleared out the thick earwax that had accumulated and dark pus that had likely come from an ear infection. The quality of hearing in my left ear remains worse than it is in my right. This probably resulted from other factors, as well.

Other than these recollections, my memory of Majori is scant, and we did not stay there long. Rose later told me that we had arrived at the home with absolutely no personal records.

The children who resided at the Majori Home had been sent there for a variety of reasons. Some were "graduates" of the Rīga Baby Home and others were there because of domestic conflicts at home.

We were compelled to move to Germany because of a secret pact that had been signed between Germany and Russia. This pact ceded the Baltic countries, of which Latvia was one, to Russia. Thus, the "invasion" of Latvia by Russian forces, on the surface, appeared to be an aggressive act of war against the German presence, but Latvians had come to trust and depend on German protection. There were two Latvian-German legions. Those Latvians, though, soon "wised up" and felt severely betrayed by the Germans. Many Latvians were hauled off to Siberia and their properties were seized. To this day, there are more Russians than Latvians in the central part of Latvia.

Within two weeks we were required to move out of the Majori

Children's Home because the Germans wanted to turn it into a hospital. One morning in the fall of 1944 (October 4 to be precise), several yellow buses arrived to take us to our next destination. I wondered where we were going next...

CHAPTER 2

STORMY CLOUDS OF WAR

The Lord will perfect that which concerns me; Your mercy, O Lord,
endures forever; do not forsake the works of your hands.
(PSALM 138:8, NKJV)

W e are His ongoing workmanship, and we were created in Christ Jesus unto good works, which God hath before ordained that we should walk in them. (See Ephesians 2:10.) Even though I am now eighty, I know that God is continuing His workmanship in my life—a workmanship that began back in those early days in Latvia. To me, even though I had no father or mother, no home, no certainty about where I was going, without any sense of security, and ominous clouds of war threatened to overwhelm me, I sensed that He was with me, and I now know He is not finished with me.

Rose/Rozīte Austrums

This kind and compassionate lady was one of five staff persons who accompanied my brother and me and 128 other orphans from the Majori Children's Home near Rīga, Latvia, to Germany. Our long and arduous journey began in 1944. She stayed with us and helped us all the way along and the entire time we were in Germany.

Most of the photos in this book were provided by her. Most of the homes where we stayed under her supervision were state-run homes for children. Rose was a high school graduate who had spent two years in undergraduate school. She had spent several summers working in summer camps for young people before she began work at Majori. It was obvious to all of us that she greatly loved children.

Rose's maiden name was Briedis. One of her classmates, Mrs. Mežaks, became a counselor at Majori, as well. Mrs. Mežaks is the one who later explained to my brother and me that we had had to go to the Baldone Children's Home because of extreme poverty. (She said, "There wasn't enough food for all of you in your home.") Later, she told us that our father had died in action in the war against the Nazis.

Rose came to America in the early 1950s, and I was able to meet with her a few times. She shared so much with me that became helpful in the compilation of this book. What a great person you were, Rose Austrums! She left for Latvia in 1997, after the death of Bernards, and died there a few years later.

Rose and Bernards Austrums, Omaha, NE, 1955

Her niece, Vija Bolin, of Omaha, Nebraska, asked me to recommend that Rose's name be included in the Jerusalem Holocaust Museum as a non-Jew who helped to rescue Jews from extermination during the Holocaust of World War II. In 2007, I learned that my brother and I may well have been two of the Jewish boys whom she saved, and I have since discovered that our names are recorded in the Holocaust Survivors' List at the National Holocaust Museum in Washington, D.C.

Rose Austrums (left) and Smaida Ašenieks (right), Omaha, NE, 1989

The others who helped us were Janīna Kurmītis who died in Canada and Alma Mežaks (wife of Jānis Mežaks) who also died in Canada. Jānis was a handsome, blond-haired, blue-eyed Aryan type who went into training to become a Nazi officer, but World War II ended before he was able to become a commissioned officer. Therefore, he became a teacher of higher-grade youths and was my teacher in Klingenberg. Another of the five women was Smaida Ašenieks, head nurse at the Majori Home. She died in Canada. The fifth woman was Alma Rāva; she remained and died in Germany.

Headed to Germany on Board a Huge Ship

So far we had traveled by horse-drawn cart, walking, and bus. Now we were getting ready to board a large ship that would take us to Germany. We waited a long time on the Rīga ship dock due to the fact that the vessel we were supposed to have taken had already embarked. While we waited, the other children played near the water, but I was afraid to do so because I could not swim and was very fearful of drowning if I fell into the water.

Our vessel was a merchant ship that was really not built to accommodate large groups of people. We slept on hastily laid out mattresses that were under the deck by the stairway (amidships). All of us were quite crowded together.

After we got situated, the ship blew its horn and sounded its deep whistle, and we began to move away from Latvia. As it did so, we started to explore the ship, and we discovered a small room with a toilet. We learned to flush the elevated tank that was near the ceiling by pulling a chain. To get to the toilet, though, we had to climb over each other. I remember when I needed to go to the bathroom in the darkness; I nearly tripped over little Augustins Viniņš. This boy had a serious ailment at this time, and he cried in pain when my foot touched his body. We learned that his illness was terminal, for he died two days later, after we disembarked from the ship at Gotenhafen, Germany.

Gotenhafen, Germany Harbor

I was becoming all too familiar with death. Tolja and I assumed that our mother must have died by this time. It was particularly disturbing that we knew children and young people who were dying, as well. Poor hygiene and a lack of nutritious food must have contributed to many of these deaths. I wondered what happened to the souls of those who died. Was there an afterlife?

Ahlbeck Children's Home

This leg of the journey was not a long boat ride (about two days). At Gotenhafen we were transferred hand over hand to a train by German sailors. We were placed in vacant boxcars. Some benches had been built for us upon which to sit down. The train took us to Ahlbeck, where we got on a bus that took us to the Ahlbeck Children's Home.

Ahlbeck, Germany, home occupied by Latvian children
when war was active, bombings, air raids, strafing, 1944

Ahlbeck is a district of the Heringsdorf municipality on the island of Usedom in the Baltic Sea. It is the easternmost of the *Kaiserbader* seaside resorts and is situated right next to the border with Poland.

Ahlbeck, Germany

This institution had been a private children's home that was run by a very sour and hard-to-get-along-with woman named Mrs. Betov. She took a dim view of us, and she insisted that only a part of the Latvian children should reside there. Even our beloved leader Rose had a hard time getting along with her.

A Nazi by the name of Mr. Bludov spent a portion of his spare time working eagerly on our behalf. Despite Mrs. Betov's protests, he was able to get most of us united at the home. A few of the children, however, had to stay in a smaller building nearby, but they were close enough to us for us all to feel that we were still together.

Mrs. Betov was disturbed by Mr. Bludov's interference, so she reported him to the German authorities. They responded by sending the man to the front lines, where he was killed. Meanwhile, Mrs. Betov continued to complain. This led the authorities to call upon a Latvian group in Germany to override her wishes. We stayed in this home throughout the winter—a challenging time due to Mrs. Betov, the harsh weather, and the war itself.

Not far from Ahlbeck was a ship-building factory, in Swinemünde. This was also a secret rocket and missile testing site of the Nazis. We all knew it could be a likely target for bombing, and a horrific attack did occur that resulted in many fatalities. So many facilities were destroyed by the relentless airplanes. Rose Austrums and several others hurried to the city to check on the home for children (babies) that was situated there.

She found that the home had suffered from a direct hit, and all the windows of the building had been shattered. Fortunately, though, the children were okay; they were found in a room playing and laughing as if nothing had happened. God has given children a remarkable capacity to enjoy the present moment and forget the past. There is so much that we can learn from their resilience, joy, and innocence.

I believe that's why Jesus said, "Let the little children come to Me, and do not forbid them; for of such is the kingdom of God" (Luke 18:16, NKJV). He loved children and He knew they have a lot to teach us.

When we first got to Ahlbeck there were not enough sheets or blankets, and so we slept on bare mattresses during nights that were very cold. We did not know where the toilet was and there seemed to be no water to drink. Consequently, on some nights the children wet their beds, and sometimes we even drank our own urine because we were so thirsty.

The smell of human excrement was everywhere, and many of us developed dysentery, which caused the problem of malodourous smells to become even worse. Our diet was scanty at best, and sometimes we would eat paper and other items because we were so hungry.

The adults would bang on large pots and pans to alert us to bombing drills. When these warnings came, we would be taken to a long tunnel under our building. The fighting was growing more intense with each passing day. I still have a vivid recollection of an afternoon when I was about to take a nap and looked out the window toward the Baltic Sea. Two small warships were engaged in a gun duel. On other days I saw warplanes shooting at overturned vessels in the sea.

During one night of heavy bombing, a German lady calmed us to sleep by singing "Brahms' Lullaby." It was very soothing and quite beautiful even though she sang in German. I will never forget the peace that her singing brought to us. She brought calmness to us even though loud explosions could still be heard. That night a building close by caught fire and burned down, but ours did not suffer any damage, except for cracked windows.

During the daytime we would frequently take walks along the seashore. In addition to some shells, we would find pieces of amber that had washed up on the shore. Latvians had long prized amber, which dripped from pine trees and would be hardened in the water over millions of years. Amber hardened into rock-like pieces, but unlike rocks, these pieces could be burned by fire. Latvians often used amber in making costume jewelry.

One vivid memory I have of this time was when I was taken to the hospital in a baby buggy, and I felt quite scared because we went past barking and snarling dogs! My stay at the hospital did not last long, however, and I was soon reunited with my brother and our friends.

To get to the cramped dining room in the basement we had to pass a large black dog. He seemed to be bigger than any of us. We never knew him to be aggressive, but my instincts told me that his behavior might be unpredictable.

Sometimes we were given special treats from a local bakery. I loved the delicious rolls and crumb cakes they brought to us. However, most of the time, our food (usually soups) left a lot to be desired. Many of us suffered from stomach pains and had to go to the hospital. I remember one time when I had horrible stomach pains and was taken to a large hospital. While there, my treatment consisted of a wet towel being placed around my abdominal area. Surprisingly, this seemed to work.

However, it was not so for a young girl who had to have her stomach pumped. She was in the bed next to mine. The medical professionals decided to perform surgery on her. When her mother came to visit her, the girl cried out, "*Mutter! Mutter!*" This puzzled me, because the Latvian word *mute* meant "mouth." Later, I realized that the girl was simply crying for her mother.

They took me along with others who were there with stomach problems to the lower floor where we were examined by a physician. They placed us on an operating table under a large, bright lamp. The idea of having to undergo an operation both fascinated and scared me, but I was glad that such a step did not have to be taken in my case.

The doctors and nurses were very kind to me, but I soon grew tired of the obnoxious hospital odors. I was so happy when a woman finally came with a case of my own clothing. I got dressed in the hallway outside my room, and, as they were discharging me, one of the nurses joked with me in a very pleasant manner. Soon thereafter I was back in the children's home, and since this was the only home I knew at the time, I was happy and relieved to be back.

Whenever we walked through the city we passed people who had large dogs. Some of these canines were larger than we were and were quite frightening to us. Many of them were German shepherds, which we had learned to respect during our time there. Fortunately, we seldom encountered a dog that displayed bad temper. It was not uncommon for us to pass Jeeps and other military vehicles wherever we went, and there were always many pedestrians as well as people on bicycles.

Time to Move On

As the sounds and sights of war drew closer, we all knew we would be moving again soon. We could see tanks and other military vehicles churning up the soil right in front of the home. We could see a military truck unloading rifles and ammunition for the soldiers in a building across the street from our building. Also, from our bedroom window we saw files of soldiers marching past and we could hear them singing familiar German marching songs. We noticed that the helmets they held in their hands were filled with bullets.

The air raids continued to increase on a daily basis. When they happened we were quickly ushered to the tunnel, which served to protect us, but at other times the tunnel was used as a form of punishment—solitary confinement for those who misbehaved. While we were there during air raids, I got a sense of what it must have been like to receive this form of punishment. It was dark, damp, smelly, and very scary. Whenever the door would be opened while we were there it was so joyful to see sunlight streaming through, cancelling out the darkness we had been experiencing.

I remember an old Latvian folk tale about men who tried to enlighten the darkness in a deep hole by means of putting the sunlight into bags and opening them below. They soon learned, though, that they reached their goal more successfully by chopping holes in the wall. We joked about this very story as we waited for the air raids to be over. Meanwhile, we were thankful we could see small streams of light shining through the cracks in the door.

We stayed indoors most of the time due to the streets being filled with soldiers and military traffic. Some people would go ice skating on nearby ponds, but there were very few civilians on the streets at this time. It seemed as if the dark clouds of war caused everyone to be frightened.

While traveling by foot in Germany during the war, we happened to take shelter for a couple of nights in an earth-covered bunker. It was filled with bunks. The German soldiers who would normally be occupying these quarters were at the battlefront. I noticed an alarm clock on a small shelf beside me. It intrigued me, and I wanted it. However, I had no luck in obtaining it as my own.

We were left to ourselves, and we heard the phone near the entryway ringing. We picked up the receiver and heard a voice asking, "*Pani mai par Ruski?*" ("Do you understand Russian?") One of us replied, "*Nyet! Nyet!*" We then hung up the phone.

We were there for a couple of days, but as we were out for a walk on a beautiful sunny day, we observed a cluster of black specks against a tall, bright, sun-lit cloud. The cluster was moving slowly to the right. While we were gawking at this spectacle, we were frightened by the sudden emergence of roaring fighter planes from the clouds above us. They were strafing our area, and bullets audibly whizzed by us and slammed into the ground all around us.

Our elders shouted, "Fall to the ground! Get down! Lie on the ground!" We did as they commanded, but as we got up to figure out what had happened, more planes descended through the clouds above us! They were shooting directly at us! This time we were commanded to jump into log-covered trenches nearby, side by side with some German soldiers. As we did so, we could hear the bullets continuing to whiz by and even slamming into the logs over our heads! Luckily, no one was hit, wounded, or killed! It is likely that the airplanes were from the Allied forces, including those of America, since we were on the ground mingling with uniformed German soldiers.

The people in charge attempted to arrange transportation for us, but to no avail. We finally walked some distance and boarded another freight train. This time we had at least two train cars to ourselves. We ate soup from milk cans and good-tasting baked goods. I remember a chubby, pleasant man who was with us.

The train moved slowly and we made several stops, usually at night.

I remember seeing tiny green and red lights by the tracks, which glowed like houses of little elves. At intersections in the cities there were luminous cylinders that were approximately three feet tall, like giant candles, minimum lighting to avoid being sighted by bombers. We slept on straw and were as crowded as sardines in a can. When we were served sausages (*desas*), we were all delighted. However, within a very short time (overnight) the sausages disappeared! They had been eaten by Vilnis Vibants, who confessed that he could not resist this temptation. Vilnis later died while in military service.

My brother Tolja spotted some butter that was stored among food items in the corner of one boxcar and slurped it up.

We stopped at a port, and we saw a locomotive being lifted aboard a waiting ship. We wondered why we were not moving. As we left our car, we noticed that our train did not have a locomotive! Was it our locomotive that had been lifted onto the ship? Whatever the case, we knew it would be quite some time before we would be moving again.

I believe we were at Stralsund. We got on horse-drawn carts in order to go to the highest place on Rügen Island. It was raining and the roads were too muddy for us to proceed. Our carts and four-horse teams got bogged down. The horses refused to go on, and some laid down in the mud. By foot we managed to make our way to a shelter near a beet field.

Again we slept on straw mattresses and we were so crowded that some of the children had to sleep literally on top of each other. Soldiers were recruited to make wooden bunk beds for us. Our food consisted of loaves of bread, vegetables, potatoes, cheese, butter, and a few other items.

Rose Austrums remembered our time in Rügen as being the worst experience of the journey. Drinking water and water for bathing had to be carried long distances through the mud, and the sleeping accommodations were horrible. Rose also remembered obtaining loaves of bread from the soldiers in exchange for packs of cigarettes.

We washed in a small tub that was filled with chilly water. In spite of this, the health of most of the children seemed good at this point. Our temporary shelter was situated on a hill that enabled those in charge to survey the entire area. I had a chat with a German youth who was the son of the owner of the beet field, and he seemed irritated that we were there. I told him not to worry, because we would be moving on soon.

Our guardians tried to secure a ship that would enable us to leave this place, but it took quite a while for them to do so. Eventually we were promised a ship, so we went to Sassnitz on the coast of Rügen, but we were disappointed once again because the ship was out in the bay and did not come in.

We had few provisions and supplies that we were able to bring with us from Majori. Food continued to be scarce, although after the other items were consumed, we had plenty of potatoes. We had gained the support of a physician named Dr. Tidriks. It was good to know that she would be able to help us if we needed her help. (This good doctor later moved to New York.)

As we continued to wait for a ship, we were seized with hunger and fear, and we were becoming desperate. There were about thirty German ships in the bay in a close cluster. They had been penned in by advancing Allies. This group of ships could have easily become a powder keg if the Allies had wanted to bombard them.

German civilians and desperate German soldiers waited to board ships to escape Russian forces that were quickly occupying the area around Berlin. This included the area over Hitler's underground bunker and command center. Our group sought to board such a ship, as well.

At last a Danish ship that was leased by the Germans arrived. As we lined up to board the ship, a German officer guarding the boarding ramp, upon seeing some of us, including my brother and me, flipped out his pistol and ordered, "Those kids are Jewish! Remove them from the line immediately!" Rose, in her take-charge-attitude, even against the Nazis, replied firmly, "No! They are NOT!" The other elders supported her statement. She said this because she feared what would happen to us if we were taken from the group. (Inwardly, though, she believed that we were Jewish. She revealed this several years later.) Because Tolja and I had no identifying documents, the women could not be accused of lying.

Believing her words, the Nazi guard let us go. We were permitted to board the ship! This episode was the closest my brother and I came to being exterminated by the Jewish Holocaust of WWII, and we owe our survival at that point to those brave women!

In subsequent documents we were listed as "Latvian Lutherans." Through DNA testing several years later, I discovered that my heritage may include a Belarussian Jewish ancestry. Recent DNA testing of other family members has revealed a similar heritage.

They kept saying that we would depart "at any minute," but Rose and a couple of others decided to take a huge gamble and return to the Rügen shelter to retrieve some of our items. They brought back with them some photos, Rose's souvenir sheet and blanket, as well as a small Latvian flag. This was a brave thing for Rose and the others to do, but they were experienced, as they knew how to twist the arms of the authorities, sometimes even altering the facts in an effort to cut red tape.

When participants in the Einsatzgruppen killer squads were later interviewed as to how they (some as young as teenagers) could mercilessly pistol-kill innocent women (some who were holding babies in their arms), causing them to fall into open pits without any seeming remorse on the part of the killers, they replied, "Oh! We simply drank more vodka and beer or took some brain-numbing drugs! No problem!"

Such intoxicants have been used throughout history, even by tribal combatants, to numb consciences, placing attackers in states of illusion and delusion. That is why I strongly urge all would-be Christian parents to keep their children from ingesting such brain-damaging toxins, at least while they are in their vulnerable, growing-up years.

Even one word that is spoken or written under such an influence disqualifies the entire message from being valid before God. (This would include all poetry that is written under those influences.) When any deviant state is accompanied by denial, we cannot respond with compassion, sympathy, empathy, patience, tolerance, or forgiveness, especially when innocents are abused, victimized, or brutalized by such behavior.

Yes, we must love the sinner, but we must also reject their sinful behavior. This is all a part of Christian parenting and role-modeling. We must reject the saying, "Do as I say, not as I do," because this is a guaranteed formula for the confusion of our children!

Fortunately, Rose and the others made it back in time to board the ship with us. I now see this as one of the many miracles we witnessed as we tried to make our escape from the dangers of the Holocaust. I don't know what might have happened if they had not returned in time.

The Danish ship was quite modern and it was filled with Nazis who were trying to escape because they knew that Germany was losing the war. Our "bedroom" was the dirty floors of the corridors. As a result, some of the children became quite sick again. It was not a very hygienic environment, that's for sure. For example, we would put our bowel movements in empty marmalade jars and toss them overboard! I was shocked when I learned that one man who had been caught stealing was shot, and his body was tossed overboard. Rose told us to get away from that area and to not even look out the window, though some children ignored her and looked anyway.

The ship we were on was trapped, in that it was unable to leave the bay. We were then transferred to one of the largest German military ships. On this ship we were able to sleep on mattresses on the floor below deck. As bunks were vacated, one by one, we were able to have our own bunks. On board with us were a group of women, other civilians, and German soldiers who had been wounded in battle.

When a bunk for me became available, I remember chatting with a soldier who let me gaze through his telescope. He seemed very kind and I remember wishing that he would give the telescope to me, but that did not happen. One danger we faced was lice infestation and the fact that a few of us had to share our bunks with others, which increased this danger.

"We Have Dying Kids on the Ship!"

We faced some of the worst living conditions on these ships—even worse than what we had experienced in the Rügen situation. We did receive help, though, from Mr. Woods, a Canadian U-boat commander who was always kind to us. The British Red Cross eventually came to our aid, as well. (During most of our stay in Germany we were under British care and guidance.)

There was no response from the Swedish Red Cross and other similar organizations. Vital goods often had to be acquired through the black market. Many of the children were sick. At Ahlbeck, Mrs. Betov had refused to provide fuel for heat. This resulted in the walls of our rooms being covered with frost. This may have caused some of the children to get kidney infections and others to develop tuberculosis. As a result, some of the sicker children were unable to leave Germany with the rest of us.

We learned that the war had ended as we heard shouts of cheer and saw rockets fired from ships. However, we remained on board the ship for several days more. Late one night we were transferred down the side of the ship to another vessel as the soldiers shined their flashlights and shouted farewells to us. We had been transferred to a filthy, single-deck cargo ship.

We were led under the deck into a room that was littered with empty cans, broken bottles, dirty rags, paper, and all sorts of other trash. Some of the children were placed in closets to make use of all available space. The horrible problem of dysentery recurred and many of us lost weight to the point of becoming quite skinny from a lack of proper nutrition. Rose told me that I had lost weight, as well, and had to be carried aboard and off one of the ships. I had been diagnosed with tuberculosis and was hospitalized twice for this disease.

While on the Danish ship we could see Sweden, but the Swedes apparently did not want to become involved with our cause. All in all, we were aboard different ships for about two weeks. During the night it was fascinating to see the lights on buoys and the flashing, bright beam of a lighthouse in the distance. Airplanes were still firing at abandoned hulks of vessels and flashes of various kinds could be seen in the sky.

During daytime the sun would reflect upon the water, and it seemed to me that there were countless flakes of gold waiting to be scooped up from the surface. My vivid imagination caused me to wonder how I could get a handful of this precious metal. I had a strong urge to jump overboard into those flakes of gold so I could grab an armful. We had heard a lot of stories about finding rich loads of gold and living happily ever after forever, but if I had jumped overboard I would have drowned!

I wondered if some of the buoys, posts, and markers might be mined, but they were apparently not, because vessels passed near or between them without being blown up.

Our counselors pleaded with British authorities by shouting from the deck, "We have dying kids on the ship!" A British officer looked us over and, being convinced of our great need, had some food sent to us. Soon thereafter we were transferred to a small ferry or tugboat. We went through a channel (the Kielisha Bucht) to Haffkrug, where the Germans were compelled to help us unload.

Rose told us that during some transfers onto or from ships, some of the children were so light in weight and emaciated, including myself, that we had to be carried by hand. I saw some of this hand-to-hand transport when we were boarding the ship at harbor in Latvia en route to Germany. Much of our traveling was done at night so as to avoid being targets of bombings.

We wandered through some bombed-out buildings on shore and were led to a place where we were sprayed with DDT powder. It was around the same time when some of the children developed measles, and one even died from this serious disease.

It was now springtime and we had endured a year-long arduous journey through the winter months. We boarded buses at Haffkrug and went on to Sierksdorf. We could sense that peace had come and the worst part of our ordeal was over. We believed that better things would soon be coming for us.

Summer home (fall to winter, 1944), Sierksdorf, Germany

Our times at the seashore in the springtime were happy and beautiful memories for the most part, but once in a while we came across dead bodies along the beach. I had never seen a dead body before. They looked like stuffed mummies to us. I'm sure these corpses had floated in from sunken ships not far from the shore. We had been warned not to get too close to these bodies, and this was not a problem for us because they were so frightening. Sometimes we would find other debris from ships, as well, such as spoons and various tools.

It had been a long war. Russia had taken over Latvia in June 1940. I had read that a secret pact between Germany and Russia regarding the Baltic States had been signed. It was likely finalized later in 1940.

The Germans ran the Russians out of the country in 1943, but in 1944, the Russians returned. Many Latvians had sided with the Germans as "the better of two evils," even though the Germans would not give them liberty. The 15th and 19th divisions of the German army were composed almost entirely of Latvians, and Mr. Austrums had served in the German army as a sergeant. He told us about one time in the war when he was in a trench, facing the Russians, and how they shouted obscenities back and forth for quite a while. He said this took place at night and we believe it was at either the Siege of Leningrad or Stalingrad.

As children, we didn't really understand the war and did not know why people were fighting. However, we regarded the Russians as the enemy and the Germans as our saviors. The Germans had, in fact, helped us considerably, and while we were living on their land we knew better than to express any kind of hostility toward them.

When we were placed under British supervision, however, we tended to regard the Germans as the defeated underdogs. Obviously, one's sentiments undergo change quickly, depending on where his bread and butter come from!

The important thing was that peace had come, and this brought joy to our hearts.

Personal Reflections

A journal is a personal record of a journey, and that's what much of this book is about. Along with the physical journey with all its pitfalls and threats, there was a spiritual journey taking place, though I didn't realize it then.

During the months we spent in transit I learned a lot about human nature. I saw many things I wish I had not seen, and I experienced many horrible and depressing things that left me wondering what life was all about.

Some good things happened during the war, as well. Some German and Dutch citizens harbored and protected Jews in their homes and elsewhere. One great example of this was the ten Boom family, which was written about in a book and movie called *The Hiding Place* by Corrie ten Boom, which I highly recommend. The entire ten Boom family, except for Corrie, ended up being killed in a concentration camp.

There are some who would deny that the Holocaust ever happened, but I am here to say that it was very real. I saw much evidence of it firsthand. The Holocaust was a genocide that took place during World War II (primarily during the years of 1941–1945), although the war had begun in the late thirties. Under Adolf Hitler and his Nazi Party more than six million European Jews (approximately two-thirds of the Jewish population in Europe at that time) were killed. Others were murdered, as well, including ethnic Poles, some Slavic groups, Soviet citizens, prisoners of war, homosexuals, Jehovah's Witnesses, Roman Catholics, black people, political opponents, and many who were physically and mentally handicapped.

As Jews were deported to ghettos and concentration camps, the Nazis were engaging in what they called "The Final Solution to the Jewish Question." In addition, paramilitary units called *Einsatzgruppen* murdered more than two million Jews through mass shootings. The total number of deaths, including Jews and the others I've mentioned, exceeded seventeen million people!

It is extremely likely that my brother and I would have been victims of the Holocaust, as well, had it not been for those adults, both Latvian and German, who came to our aid by protecting us from the Nazis and other extreme dangers. Our protectors were brave and strong, and because of them I am still here today.

Had the authorities learned about the likelihood of our Jewish identity, my brother and I might well have ended up on a train to Auschwitz! As I consider this, I find myself rejoicing over the faithfulness of our God and the helpfulness of the many, like Rose, who constantly looked after our needs.

CHAPTER 3

A WHOLE NEW BEGINNING

Blessed be the God and Father of our Lord Jesus Christ,
who has blessed us with every spiritual blessing in
the heavenly places in Christ.

(EPHESIANS 1:3, NKJV)

The circumstances of my life thus far had been most difficult and trying. However, as a little boy, I did not really know how bad things were for us. The truth is I had nothing with which to compare my life. I know I daydreamed of better times and hoped for the best. Never once did I lose hope, and I believe this came from God. I was not bitter about the things that had happened to me.

In this chapter you will learn about how things began to change for us as peace came to Europe and to our own hearts. Many of the children we were with had already been adopted, and Tolja and I wished for the same. The peace that came to Europe filtered into our own hearts, and life began to change for us in dramatic ways.

A Taste of Family Life

The first obvious sign to me that peace had come was when we were approaching Haffkrug, and I noticed a large, rusty ship. Instead of guns blazing from the boat, I saw people sunbathing and hanging out their laundry on deck. It was definitely a peaceful scenario. Our next stop was Sierksdorf, a place where some of us could start planting our feet on the ground. It was springtime in 1945. Sierksdorf is a municipality in the district of Ostholstein in Schleswig-Holstein. It is situated on the Bay of Lübeck.

Our group occupied seven summer homes in Sierksdorf. One of these was very nice indeed. It was owned by an attorney and it was filled with fine furniture, including a piano. Rose suggested to the lawyer that he should probably relocate some of the furniture, and he wisely did so. For more than a month my brother and I stayed in a simpler house to the west of the nicer one, along the coast of the Baltic Sea.

We slept on mattresses on the floor, and the home was quite crowded. While we were in this house we met the Brüders family. This wonderful family "adopted" a number of us as part of their own family. It was more of a foster arrangement than actual adoption, but it was nice to be part of such a large family. Through much of my time in Germany I enjoyed family life with the Brüderses and later on with Miss Marta Bulova, who went on to marry Mr. Richards, the British head of the Rohlsdorf home.

Brüders family, 1952

After we were somewhat settled, Mr. Brüders built some double bunk beds for us, which meant that we no longer had to sleep on mattresses on the floor. One night, while sleeping on the top bunk, I fell off and landed on the floor on my back. I thought I was about to die because the air had been completely knocked out of me and it was awhile before I could breathe again. I began to cry, but Mrs. Brüders picked me up and spoke reassuring words to me.

She took me over to the windowsill where she held me on her lap. At that moment I felt quite loved and it brought back memories of when my mother used to hold me and comfort me. Soon I was back in bed and back to normal.

The next day Mr. Brüders built side rails on the top bunk to prevent a similar occurrence. He was a very talented man. We later called him *Tēvs*, a word similar to "dad." I remember how he would smoke eels atop a barrel. He would start a fire and put iron rods through the heads of the eels, which would often squirm in their crates, and then he would suspend them into a thick column of smoke within the barrel. By using an umbrella he would even do this on rainy days. The freshly smoked eels tasted delicious, far better than those one buys in the marketplace. Mr. Brüders also had a team of workhorses that he would use for various purposes. I wouldn't go near them, though, because they were very temperamental and would sometimes become quite vicious toward each other.

A wooden stairway led to the seashore where we would sometimes go to play and walk to the dwellings of other children who were located not far away. Unfortunately, many corpses washed ashore and we were reminded of the horrors of war. I remember how some men came with a wheelbarrow, into which they would place a body, and they buried some in a rough grave not far from the wooden stairway. This made the seashore a lot less appealing to us, so we would not go there as often as before.

Not far from a hedge that overlooked the sea, some men built a latrine for us. It was of a simple design. First, they dug a large hole in the ground and over it they placed a long, many-holed board for our use when we had to go to the bathroom. It was here that we learned that our feces were filled with white, wiggling worms! I wondered if they were devouring our insides. Eventually we were treated for this condition and we no longer saw worms in our feces.

School Days

After a month or so we moved into a larger house farther back from the shore. It was almost directly behind the house where we had stayed earlier, which was now an office for British officials. After we moved here we began going to a small country school—a one-room school that was painted white. While there, we dabbled in art a bit, and I spotted a sheet with an impression of a fish on it. I traced its outline with a pencil, and the woman who was there complimented me for my fine drawing. One of the sons of the Brüderses happened to be passing by at the same time, and he expressed great pleasure with my work, as well.

Unfortunately, it was not possible for us to continue at this school due to the cold weather that was coming in. We were given a physical checkup by a local doctor, who estimated my age to be about seven years old. I was then placed in the second grade together with Jānis Brüders, a son of the couple who were taking care of us. Our teacher was Mr. Rītiņš, whose name meant "morning." He was a middle-aged, one-legged man with a kind disposition and a good education.

He noticed that I could read relatively well, and the chief book we had for reading was the New Testament of the Holy Bible. Mr. Rītiņš later moved to Canada with his wife, but while he was in Sierksdorf he taught us several subjects, such as biology. He said that if we eat too many plum stones or cherry pits, they might become lodged in the finger of our intestines—the appendix. If this were to happen, he explained, the resulting infection could well become fatal. To support this theory, he drew a primitive diagram. What he said seemed quite reasonable to us.

On the way to school one morning we managed to get hold of some of Mr. Brüders' freshly smoked fish and quickly devoured them, but this slowed us down some so we were late for school. Mr. Rītiņš did not like tardiness, so he was quite displeased with us for being late.

In school we learned a variety of things. As winter began, we learned about the nature and purpose of thermometers, observed the process of combustion, and we watched a lighted candle floating on a piece of wood in a pan of water and then being enclosed in a jar, thereby extinguishing the flame. Mr. Rītiņš had a small figure of a man on a pedestal balancing a turning and swinging bar, which was weighted at both ends. It was fascinating to watch this during our classes.

We also learned simple arithmetic, spelling, and oral reading. A lot of what we did would be considered rote learning, so I remember very few specifics about it. The home in which our classes were held was the residence of another group of children who were supervised by a very strict woman, who would not tolerate any foolishness. Therefore, things were usually pretty quiet there.

Eventually we began attending classes in a different building—a brick house, and around the same time we moved into a different residence—a larger house with a thatched roof. The Brūderses remained as "our parents" and they were very loving and concerned about each of us. The largest room in the house served as our playroom and dining room. There was an electric outlet in this room, and I did not know what it was for. However, I soon learned what it was for when out of curiosity I placed a small metal spring into the socket. The coil became red-hot and singed the tips of my fingers. The scars from that learning experience lasted a good long while, but I had learned my lesson.

We learned that *Tēvs* had stored several interesting items in the attic, including belongings from the Brūders family and his brass lantern. He promised that we would inherit these things when he died. Sad to say, I wanted to inherit those heirlooms soon! We knew that one of us would inherit his traditional, worn, gray, flat hat that was typical of peasant folk in Europe at this time. This type of hat is still worn in Europe today.

Tēvs, as you know, was our fatherly provider. He would always talk about his age and accomplishments, his work, and his horses. He had given special names to his horses, and he hoped we would all ride them and work with them as we grew older. Even though these horses were somewhat wild and would run away from time to time and have to be rounded up, we regarded them as members of the family. *Tēvs* had such a positive attitude about his horses, and this caused us to like them, as well.

Birthday Parties

One day I watched Mrs. Brūders as she made a very fancy, multi-layered cake. Its rich frosting was a mixture of soft butter and some kind of berry jam. She applied the frosting with a cloth "cone." We didn't know what this cake was for, and she told us it was a torte (a very rich Latvian cake that was baked with heavy dough that consisted of lots of eggs).

As we were seated at the table that evening, *Tēvs* announced that the cake was to help us celebrate the birthday of a friend whom we all knew well. At first, we did not know who he was referring to, but when we saw the skillful design of a horse on the cake, we had a clue. It was one of the horses' birthdays! We chuckled as we realized for whom the cake was. Though it seemed a bit strange that we would celebrate the birthday of a horse, it was clear to us that *Tēvs* greatly valued them as his means of livelihood and transportation.

The cake had candles on it and we sang the usual birthday song, then we enjoyed the torte. It tasted wonderful, and I don't recall having anything like it until many years afterward. Eventually (in 1950) my brother and I were adopted by an American couple—Rev. and Mrs. Victor Boe. On the tenth anniversary of our adoption, I asked Mrs. Alberta Jurjans of Fargo, North Dakota, to make a very fancy whipping cream and strawberry-covered, multilayered torte. It, of course, had to be refrigerated and was an American version of the Latvian original.

My mother and father thought the cake was too rich, so this was the last time for quite a while that I would be able to enjoy such a delicacy.

As you might imagine, we ate well in Mrs. Brūders' kitchen. She would serve us wonderful meals of meat, potatoes, gravy, vegetables, soup, and the like. At other times we would simply have jam or jelly sandwiches. I was happy that she introduced us to a very tasty bread spread known as marmalade, which was made from orange peelings. To this very day I enjoy the taste of marmalade.

Birthdays were a great cause for celebration. When one of the children would have a birthday we would all get together for a party. This would include children from other homes, as well. A variety of gifts would be given to the guest of honor, and everyone would grow excited as they thought about their own birthday and the party they would have. However, I worried a bit about the fact that my birthday was unknown.

On one occasion during the autumn, I was appointed to represent our home at a birthday party that was going to be held in a smaller home not far away. It was near the sea. I was given a small present to take with me. One other boy accompanied me, and I remember that we ate orange berries and fruits that we found along the way. (These were filled with tiny spikes but were very sweet.) The room where the party was held was quite dark and few were present. However, it was a very friendly and joyous atmosphere.

Medical Care

A doctor (who may have been Dr. Tidriks who helped us in Rügen) visited our home quite often. She would give us periodic checkups. I remember her jabbing her hypodermic needle into our hips, and as a result, many of us could not sit comfortably for several days afterward. Sometimes these areas would become infected and she would have to give us antibiotic medications.

Even though the doctor would not stay long after administering her various procedures, we got to know her well. She was a medium-height, husky, businesslike woman, but when she would come to take care of us she would always bring us candy and chocolate—a good way to win over kids, that's for sure. She was always very faithful in attending to our physical and medical needs.

Discoveries

The room where we had been sleeping had been converted into living quarters for the Brūders family so we had to move to a different room. One day we noticed a strong, unpleasant aroma that was wafting into our room from the outside. *Tēvs* explained what it was. He had installed a gasoline-powered pump for sewage disposal. The sewage emptied into a freshly dug, open trench. It was like other ones I'd seen in other homes.

Windows in most of the homes we occupied were not airtight, so during windy and stormy days we could always hear the howling of the wind. Sometimes we imagined it was the sound of an owl, a wolf, or a threatening beast. Most disturbing indeed!

Some of the ladies would come over to our house in the evenings once in a while to do knitting and dressmaking, and to chat with one another. These "gab sessions" would last late into the night. One night as I went to the chamber pot to relieve my bladder, I noticed that the light was still on in the other room and I could hear the ladies chatting. All of a sudden, however, I heard a small pop-like explosion and the light went out. The two women who remained got up and screamed in panic. What had happened was that the lightbulb that was above them had burst! When they realized what had happened, they came back, replaced the bulb, and continued what they were doing. Having enjoyed watching this spectacle, I returned to bed.

On another evening, a German neighbor observed some small vessels congregating in the bay. He ran to our house and advised us to turn off our lights, for fear that we might soon be under attack. We blocked out the light by placing a blanket over the window that faced the sea, but we kept our lights on. The next morning we were relieved to see that the vessels were gone.

This event may have been responsible for some nightmares I had afterward. In one of these horrific dreams I was gobbled up by a wolf, but awoke just before I was totally swallowed! Another nightmare involved heavy rain with thunder and intermittent flashes of lightning. I was fascinated by this thunderstorm, so I tried to open the door to go out-side. As I did so, I was thrown outside by the wind's force and found myself flailing about in the mud and greatly frightened by the thunder and lightning.

The next night I had a similar dream, but in this one, though I was hurled outside once again, I somehow managed to climb into an open wooden barrel in which I rolled around and around until I came to a stop by a stone cistern where some young people were chatting. Then the dream was over; it had ended on a much more positive note than the previous one had.

In a later dream I experimented with reality in order to find if I was really dreaming, by closing my eyes in the dream to see if all would be dark or whether something else would appear. Nothing appeared, how-ever, except for a faint light.

I found this conscious awareness during dreams quite fascinating. When things went unusually well, I hoped and hoped that I was not dreaming! When things were not going well I hoped I was dreaming. If some of the things we dream about actually occurred in real life, we would be haunted with unbearable guilt and fear. It is definitely fortunate that in our public conduct our actions are not as spontaneously controlled by the fluctuations of desire that we experience in dreams.

We took frequent walks in the area. As we walked, we had an oppor-tunity to learn about our environs. About half a mile to the west, there was a small cluster of farmhouses and barns where a small group of Germans lived and worked. Just to the south, there were several houses that were occupied by Polish families. One of these people came to our house angrily after one of the boys had thrown sticks at him. We were strongly warned never to do this again, and I'm fairly certain we all com-plied with this directive.

Language barriers between us and the Germans and others didn't help the situation, either. It is hard to be neighborly when it is impossible to communicate.

As we walked along the road toward the east we encountered a dung-covered, plowed-up field and an abandoned military vehicle. We ended up at a small railway station where we observed long trains moving eastward. The train cars were loaded with military vehicles, including tanks, and this made us wonder if the war was really over as we had been told.

In the springtime we celebrated the *Līgo* festival not far from the seashore. The children sang folk songs and danced to them. We also played games. In one of the games we would move around in a circle and hold each other's ears. It actually made me sick to experience the greasy feel of another person's ears. The girls who danced in the *Līgo* festival wore beautiful costumes; there was a festive spirit in the air. Young and old alike loved this festival, which had plenty of food and other forms of enjoyment. We gathered some plums from a nearby tree, which we greatly enjoyed. We sang songs as we shared these with others.

While we were at this site, the British gave us a thorough DDT-powder treatment. The large gasoline engines that sprayed the powder roared loudly, and this made the experience somewhat exciting.

A New Home in Haffkrug

Haffkrug, Germany, is situated in Ostholstein, Schleswig-Holstein, along the seashore. It has long been a popular vacation spot for Germans and others.

As I mentioned before, the homes we were staying in were summer homes, so it was apparent that we could not long endure the cold of winter in those buildings. *Tēvs* tried to keep the small wood-burning stove going and he kept the supplies of wood well-stocked. Nonetheless, the time had come for the children to be taken to new homes. Many of them moved to Hamburg, into a large building where they were befriended by a policeman.

I observed that the nearby Polish families were also in the process of moving. Hence, the trucks kept coming and leaving to take people to different places where it was warmer. Soon after our celebration of

Christmas that year it was clear that we would be moving, too. Winter had definitely arrived. I remember walking over cracking ice that had formed atop small puddles.

I was quite overjoyed when Jānis Brūders gave me his flashlight that had long fascinated me. It had a magnifying lens that had red and green filters. The only problem was that it did not have any batteries. I ended up discarding it when we moved to the next place because I could not afford batteries. Nonetheless, I was grateful to him because I know he wanted me to remember him. Though he was a few years older than me, we had gotten to know each other pretty well.

According to Rose, we had arrived in Sierksdorf in early May. This accounts for the late spring/early summer *Līgo* festival I referred to earlier as well as the fall *Līgo* festival, which was also known as the harvest festival (when we shared the plums with others). Some of the children had left for Hamburg around the end of September 1945, and most of them would be reunited with us at Malente in February or March of 1946.

A few of us, including my brother and me, went to Haffkrug sometime in October or November of that year. This was not too far from our last home in Sierksdorf. Our new home was a single-story building in the heart of the town. Our house faced the Baltic Sea, and we often watched sailboats and larger vessels as they plied the waters. One ship would weigh anchor almost straight out from our house. We would take frequent walks along the seashore, but the temperatures became too cold for us to do this often. We noticed a number of fishermen's boats and net-drying racks. Some boats were wrecked and rotten while others were being repaired or touched up.

We missed our last home and the Brūderses who had truly been wonderful to us. It seemed as if we had become like nomads, moving from place to place, but in the process I learned a lot and I do not regret all the moves we had to make. Our new counselor was a lady who told us that Latvia was known for its dairy industry.

One point of frustration for me was that I had never learned to tie my shoes. The shoes I wore had always had buckles on them, so there was no need to know how to tie laces. I never really got the hang of this until a few years later, I'm sorry to say.

Tolja and I walked at least twice to a large theater that was not too far away. Once while we were there we saw a production of one of the Grimm Brothers' fairy tales, *Jack and the Beanstalk*. Except for my brother and me, the theater was almost empty. There were many things in this theater that fascinated me. One was the flying unicorn on the red-cloth mantle above the stage. I also enjoyed the many-colored lights that were along the outer rim of the stage.

As we left the theater, we noticed a Latvian flag flying atop a building. Not far from there we saw several cows grazing in a pasture, and we remembered the words of our counselor, that the Latvians had fine cows and a great dairy industry.

Many British trucks were in this area, and the personnel seemed to have great difficulty getting them started in the cold weather. We saw that many of the hoods of these vehicles were open as the men examined their engines. I hoped that I might be able to have free reign with one of these trucks, especially if it was totally out of commission. I wanted to examine its parts and learn about mechanics. Unfortunately, that day never came.

Another Moving Day

Another move was in the offing, this time to Neustadt or a small farming community not far from there. When we got there we saw a large body of water, which we assumed was a part of the Baltic Sea. If my memory serves me correctly, we stayed at this new place until spring.

There was a teeter-totter outside, and Tolja and I used it soon after we saw it. It was great fun. There was a small dock close by, from which we were able to catch tiny minnows with our bare hands. Under supervision, we would take our noon naps in a shelter that had torn and mice-eaten mattresses. Between the shelter and our home was a large tree with a thermometer on it. We soon took the thermometer down and tore it apart. In this way we were learning about our world and how things work.

I found a small reed section of a harmonica in the dirt, and to my delight, I discovered that it worked. One of the boys found a gas mask, and I was eager to get my hands on it, so I could investigate how it worked. However, the supervisor took it and threw it into the latrine. I decided not to jump in and get it, considering all the smelly waste products that were there.

Across the sea to the north we could hear deep, booming sounds, and we wondered what they were. These would be followed by columns of smoke, as if practice bombings were taking place. Even to our south we could hear similar explosions, which we understood were probably coming from the Russian sector. Hearing these sounds made me shudder with fear because I certainly did not want to see any of us go through another war, which would mean another difficult and challenging flight to another safe place. Such a thought was very terrifying to me, so I immediately dismissed it.

The road to the west side of the house turned westward along the shore. It was always a relief to me not to run into Russian soldiers while walking along this road. On the other side of the road was a hill that had several small evergreens. They grew close together and this provided hiding places for all sorts of strange animals with which I was not familiar. I think my imagination even created some of these!

My vivid imagination envisioned these animals leaping out after me. That's why I avoided taking this walk after dark. The road went uphill to a place where the children would be able to pick some cattails near the water. From time to time we would see a man with a horse-drawn carriage pass us. He was not friendly and I suspected him of being a Russian spy. Whenever I saw him, I would try to avoid him.

On the east side of the house, there was another road that went along the edge of a small lake. About one-fifth of a mile down that road was a rickety wooden bridge, and there were beautiful evergreens along the way. We chopped down one of these evergreens for our Christmas tree. At the top of the hill, among some very tall pine trees, we found an abandoned military tank. One of its treads had been broken off and its turret was resting upon partly uprooted trees.

If I hadn't been so closely supervised, I'm sure I would have spent hours exploring this tank. I wanted to examine its engine, but this desire was never satisfied. Among the trees we discovered empty shells and unfired casings of bullets as well as a lot of metal scrap from military equipment of all sorts.

We felt that we would encounter Russians if we went much farther. However, we did follow a small stream toward the direction where we thought they were situated. We never did see any Russians, though, and I was greatly relieved that this was so.

Going northward, the road passed a small cow pasture and a white church. We could hear its bell every Sunday morning, but I don't believe we ever entered it. We did, however, play on its lawn quite frequently. I felt a desire to go to church to see what it was like, but we never did so.

Several other buildings, mostly small farmhouses and outbuildings, were located along the road. At one of the farmhouses we encountered some geese that would come out and snap at us! Several rusted-out cars (some painted with camouflage paint) were parked along the way. Most of these appeared to be disabled. I snatched a hose from the engine of one of these and blew through it on the way home. The supervisor subsequently removed it from me, because, he said, it was dirty.

A side road to the north led past a seemingly abandoned stone church that had beautiful stained-glass windows. It was hidden by some trees. A large hog shed nearby could be heard and smelled from a distance. Not far from this spot, there was a blueberry patch that we frequently visited for berry picking.

In shallow water just to the north I saw what looked like a broken-in-two fuselage of a bomber. I thought that one day I might wade out to it in order to examine it. Then I thought there might be dead soldiers in it, and this discouraged me a bit. The fact that there might be rifles within the plane, though, piqued my interest, and my curiosity about it burned brightly for a long time afterward.

It seemed that my interest in how things work and mechanics in general might lead me to pursue this field of endeavor as either a vocation or an avocation. I still have a great interest in these things even though I eventually became a pastor.

The Latvian word for airplane is *lidmašīna*, and while the war was raging, hearing airplanes overhead brought great fear to me. Distant beats would come closer and closer and then merge into a loud, steady roar of engines until they passed overhead and gradually faded away. The sounds of the *lidmašīna* no longer affected me in the same way, for I knew that those sounds were no longer omens of frightful destruction. In early 1949, in Hamburg, Germany, I finally went aboard an airplane and my fear of them greatly diminished at that time.

I remember one time, when we were on our way to Rīga from Baldone, that we had observed an airplane circling overhead and going around and around as if its steering mechanism had become stuck! This was a weird feeling and some of us wondered if we were being spied upon in preparation for an attack! Some of these planes left vapor trails in the sky in small dashes, as if they were sending a coded message.

Most of my memories of planes, though, are associated with Ahlbeck, for there was rarely a night there when planes could not be heard, and every plane was a potential bearer of destruction to our home and our very lives.

Well, the time came for us to get ready to move once more, and not many days before our departure several of the children were able to go to a circus in a nearby city. Two of us could not go because we were sick. We decided to have our own "circus" by catching a mouse and tying a string to one of its hind legs. It frantically ran around the room in an effort to get free. One of our counselors thought this was cruel, and he made us throw the animal into a waste barrel, which seemed to me to be even more cruel!

Sensing that we had missed out on something, the chief driver for the home gave each of us an opportunity to accompany him in his truck on his trips to get milk from a nearby dealer.

Later, we took a more interesting trip to a large city, which I now believe was Berlin. The driver had gone here to spend some time with an old friend. In order to do so, we had to take a streetcar part of the way. There was a narrow canal along the way. Near the city we noticed the rusted hulls of many ships in this canal. I noticed that some of these ships were being hoisted to the shore where repair efforts were taking place. We had fun climbing an observation tower until we got to the top, where we found that many people had deposited their excrement there!

Our driver's friend lived in an apartment and he gave us a very cheery greeting upon arrival. He took me in his arms and rocked me like a baby. This seemed a bit strange and uncomfortable to me. I was not used to being held by anyone.

We noticed some street barricades being erected and we assumed that beyond those barriers was the Russian sector of the city. It was very enjoyable to be in such a large city and to see so much. I was very grateful that the driver took us there.

It was early March, and our next home was to be in Malente, Germany.

Personal Reflections

Germany had become our home for the time being, and most of the German people treated us nicely. We knew that the Germans had been largely responsible for World War II and that they had lost the war, but that was pretty much the extent of what we knew at that time.

Our nomadic existence, though challenging, had taught us many things about people and places. We realized that we might have to move without any notice at any given time, and this gave life a feeling of uncertainty. We knew that the friendships we made and the places we enjoyed could be easily taken away, so we were afraid to "put down roots."

That the war was over and peace had come was wonderful news to us. Tolja and I remained hopeful that we would one day be adopted, maybe by Americans, but it would be a few years before that would happen.

As human beings, we can experience several kinds of peace, such as peace of mind, inner peace, spiritual peace, peaceful relationships, and peace after war.

> Jesus said, "Peace I leave with you, My peace I give to you; not as the world gives do I give to you. Let not your heart be troubled, neither let it be afraid".
>
> (JOHN 14:27, NKJV)

I learned this verse by heart years later. Now I know that the peace Jesus gives is perfect peace, a supernatural peace that surpasses all understanding. Tolja and I were experiencing a bit of this as we realized the difference between war and peace, and felt grateful that the war was over.

CHAPTER 4

MALENTE

And we know that all things work together for good to those who love
God, to those who are the called according to His purpose.
(ROMANS 8:28, NKJV)

Life is an adventure that never ends. There are discoveries and reve-
lations all along the way. In this chapter I share some of the things I
learned and experienced during my brief stay in the city of Malente. Things
for me were becoming more peaceful and stable, and I was enjoying life
with relatively little fear. I was beginning to develop relationships with
both children and adults, and in general, I was feeling happy and hopeful.

It seemed as if my curiosity knew no bounds. I wanted to learn about
the world, how things worked, plants, animals, people, and myself. Each
day seemed like a new opportunity to learn. The walks we took, the parties
we enjoyed, and even the classroom opened new vistas of understanding
for me. I was excited to be alive and I wanted to make the most of my life.

Easter in Our New Home

Evidence of springtime could be seen everywhere as we settled in at
Malente. This municipality is in the district of Ostholstein, in Schleswig-
Holstein, Germany. It is close to Eutin and Lübeck.

Daffodils were in bloom and robins were searching for worms in the soft earth. Easter came and a short person who was dressed up like a bunny leapt atop the tables in front of us, causing us to be very delighted and excited. After the white, fuzzy bunny was finished with entertaining us, we enjoyed painted Easter eggs, candy, and a special meal.

At first there were paintings of battleships on the dining room wall, but those works of art were being replaced by a mural that showed various fairy-tale characters gathered around a table. It was very interesting to watch the artist as he did his work while we ate. He sketched the outline of each figure with charcoal first and then filled the spaces with bright colors. He included various animals in the scene as well, including giraffes and elephants, and we were thrilled to see each one make its appearance on the wall.

Children from Hamburg were also there, and we enjoyed sharing our experiences with them and learning about what they had been through. We were all glad to be together.

Malente, Germany

Malente, Germany, 1946, photo from Mr. Ronald Yeats, England,
Tolja in front 2nd from left, Volodja to Tolja's left, Note star of David
on arm of man on the right, one of these photos has larger field of view
but seems of lesser quality

A Hospital Stay

Not long after arriving in Malente I had to go to the hospital, but I did not know why. It was a large hospital in Schlutup, not far from a harbor where much shipping was done. I could see large construction cranes moving back and forth. I also noticed a streetcar, which made its regular stops in this area and then raced onward. I could hear the deep and mournful sound of a ship's horn from time to time. At night I could see sparks flying from the streetcar's contact with its cable as it sped past the hospital, and I could hear the rhythmic clatter of its wheels. All of this was new and fascinating to me.

They put me in a small room on the third floor of the hospital. Some other boys and I got into some mischief by tearing apart the telephone fixtures and electrical connections in this room. This caused several of us, myself included, to be transferred to a large room nearby. My bed was next to the crib of a little girl who cried most of the time. Even after her mother and father had come to visit her, she was inconsolable, temperamental, and uncooperative. I felt bad for her and hoped she would stop crying soon. Eventually they moved her to a different location.

The other boys and I continued to be challenging rascals. One example of this was when a telephone on a windowsill rang. No one answered, so a boy who was in a bed across from me asked the boy who was next to him to hand him the receiver. The other boy attempted to do so, but the cord wouldn't reach. In his attempt to take the phone to his friend, the telephone fell off the windowsill and onto the floor. It cracked open and the bell made some muffled sounds for a few seconds. I went to the phone in the hope of being able to dismantle it and see how it worked. Soon, however, a repairman arrived and fixed the phone. It was put back on the windowsill, but it was totally removed from that location some time later.

The children across the room from me were receiving their smallpox vaccinations, which consisted of a lot of little pricks in the skin of their arms. I'm pretty sure I had been vaccinated already and this made me feel greatly relieved, because it seemed as if the other children were going through a very painful procedure as evidenced by their loud cries and screams.

The nurses took blood samples from us by piercing our earlobes with pins or small shards of glass and putting the blood that was drawn on small plates of glass. It was not until much later that they used the automatic, spring-operated piercing mechanisms, which were psychologically more bearable.

While I was at the hospital one of the nurses introduced us to an electronic device that was used to exercise our muscles. It consisted of a small, portable mechanism in a black case. The device had an arm band that was a strip of dampened cloth that was connected to wires. She had each of us try out this machine. I remember when the band was put on the arm of one of the boys, his fingers opened and closed in a rhythmic manner. I don't know for sure, but he may have been controlling these movements on his own, at least a bit.

Perhaps out of fear I did not want to try out the machine, so I sat on a table in my pajamas as the nurse sketched a picture of me. She did the same with another boy, but we never got to see those sketches. Sketching other people became something I enjoyed doing, as well, especially when I moved to the United States.

The automatic flush mechanism of the toilet (kloset) fascinated me. It was the kind of toilet that uses no water tank but is operated by a lever attached to the water pipe at the back of the toilet. This kind of toilet is still used in many places today.

At the end of the building was a stack of oxygen tanks, which looked a bit like bombs to me. At first, I thought they were bombs. A bit farther on was the dentist's office. He used a foot-operated, flywheel type of drill, which produced sounds that scared many of us, but it did its job. He used a white compound to fill cavities. Because I was fascinated by his equipment, I didn't really mind going to the dentist, but a lot of my friends did.

Just before I left the hospital I was moved to a nearby barracks, and this gave me greater liberty to walk around the premises. Though we longed to return "home," we enjoyed good food and excellent attention while we were in the hospital. It was wonderful to finally get outside and play in the parking area nearby and to enjoy the many blessings of nature once more.

Back to the Hospital

Soon after my return to Malente I had to go back to the Schlutup Hospital. Again, the reason why I had to go there was unknown to me. Perhaps they wanted to monitor me in light of the tuberculosis I had contracted sometime before.

This time I was in a different room that had a small handcrafts shop within it. I saw hammers, saws, boards, paints, crayons, sketching paper, and other such items there. One of the boys in the room was quite artistic. He could sketch trees and shrubs with remarkable skill, and he could make animals and other figures out of clay. Though I tried to imitate him, I soon realized he was much more talented than me. He was also a great storyteller, and I believe he sensed that I was quite gullible in that I believed many of his stories. He told of a time when he had gone for a walk in the woods and was attacked by a pack of wolves! He told how he climbed a tree to get away from them, but the wolves pursued him up the tree by climbing on top of each other. One of the wolves was able to grab hold of his foot when he remembered that he had a whistle with him. He used the whistle to call for help. His father came to his assistance and killed all the wolves! As hard as it was to believe his story, I thought he was telling me the truth.

A boy who was heavily drugged and quite banged up was placed in the bed next to mine. As he emerged from his drugged state, he began to whimper and groan as if he was in severe pain. I learned later that he had fallen from quite a height and had badly fractured his limbs. A number of doctors and nurses took care of him and it was not long before they moved him to a different place.

One afternoon, a small shack nearby caught on fire, causing a column of black smoke to ascend into the air. This caused a great disturbance, and while the fire was being tended to they had a fire drill for the whole hospital. They removed me to a temporary location until everyone was sure that all danger had past.

I noticed how many adults were listening to the radio, and this was something I had never seen before. From my hospital bed, I could see adults sunbathing on the roofs or porches of their apartment houses. I could also see evidence of logging in the distance.

When I was in the hospital the first time, I had looked out my window and wondered if I would get badly hurt if I jumped out to the pavement below. I saw many small evergreens that I thought would cushion such a fall. Then, during my second stay there, I examined the scene a little more carefully and noticed that there were deep depressions in the ground, so a fall from the window would have been quite likely fatal. I was glad I never attempted such an act.

However, one of the boys, Jānis Puķīte, actually did jump out of the third-story window to his death! This horrendous tragedy caused the hospital to put steel bars in the windows of the children's units. The Rohlsdorf Children's Home took the same precautions, and these measures prevented anyone from leaping out of the windows.

In the shop section of our area, I noticed that one of the instructors was building a large, fancy airplane. It had four propellers. I found his work to be utterly fascinating and I tried to make my own, but without success.

Not long thereafter my counselor came to take me back to Malente. She kindly brought a large bag of candy with her. I was thrilled to know I would be returning home, and equally thrilled to have such delicious candy. The shop instructor had finished his airplane and painted it red. He then gave it to me as a farewell gift. I was delighted to receive his handiwork and showed it off when I got back to Malente.

My first stay at the hospital lasted about three weeks, and the second stay was about two weeks.

Malente

The city of Malente is located between two lakes—Kellersee and Dieksee. We would take walks around this beautiful area both within the city and its outskirts. There was a park not far from the home where we would go for outings and picnics.

We noticed that large powered rafts and small barges would come to the dock to pick up a load of war veterans. Most of these men wore pajama-like, striped garments and were most likely released prisoners of war. Their destination was a small island to the north of our home. During the summer some veterans could be seen lying in the sun. A number of them were amputees—a gruesome sight indeed.

There was a large hospital not far from the home, which was likely a veterans' hospital. Some of our children were sent there sometimes for minor ailments. When they returned, they would report that they had seen men whose faces were badly disfigured, some without ears or noses. Veterans with a black patch over one eye were common sights there.

There was a concrete embankment along part of the lake on which we would walk from time to time. The water on the other side was usually shallow, but we would often see a number of snakes swimming there. I had a great fear of snakes at the time (and still do), so I was never thrilled to see them there and always tried to avoid them.

Once we came upon a small porcupine on the right of the trail. The animal had rolled up into a ball and acted as if it were dead, probably out of fear of us. Some of the children kicked it out of curiosity, but most of us just left it alone. A bit farther along the trail we noticed a court that had been used either for tennis or volleyball. It was in a deteriorated state. Weeds were growing all around it and through the cracks in the concrete. To me, this was a sad sight to see, because I realized people used to have fun there and now they could not.

As we kept walking, we came to a sandy beach that had springs bubbling up through the sand. We often played on the beach, which was situated on one of the lakes I mentioned earlier. Eventually this became a public beach with a large diving platform. From then on we were forbidden from entering it; the whole area was enclosed by a wire fence.

We found other places for swimming, however, and summer was filled with great fun and excitement when we stayed at Malente. Sometimes we would take long walks along the railroad tracks. We would follow the tracks eastward for some distance. Now and then a small workman's car would be seen scooting by us and kicking up the leaves behind it.

At times we would see single rail cars that were propelled by two men alternately pushing up and down on a large lever. These cars could not move too fast, but we knew the men would go long distances, especially when they had extra men riding along.

In the woods that were south of the tracks we noticed a few large granite monuments that were dedicated to some heroes. Their condition made it seem as if they had been forgotten. About half a mile east of Malente we crossed the tracks and played in a small opening among the trees. We turned over rotten stumps and logs and discovered various kinds of insects (wasps, ants, bees, and worms) and flowers.

Malente, Germany, children on walk collecting wood, likely spring 1946,
Volodja on woman's lap, Tolja 2nd to Volodja's right

To the south of our home was an old but still operating flour mill that was powered by a stream that turned a large wheel. From time to time we would see an old truck that brought bags of unground grain to the mill and took bags of finished flour from it. Beyond this site there were beautiful private homes that were nicely landscaped.

We would climb a hill and walk along its crest among scattered evergreens. Small dragonflies that were bluish-green in color would fly near us. We also saw a variety of butterflies, mayflies, lady bugs, horseflies, and other flying insects. As we proceeded, we would find ourselves in the midst of stinging nettle, something we eventually learned to stay away from, along with other prickly weeds, thistles, and the like. We knew that if we remained on the trail, we would not be bothered by these troublesome plants.

We came upon a pair of small tracks just south of the home. Here we saw a chain of tiny gravel cars that were pulled by a small locomotive. In all likelihood the gravel was used for cement mixing. Beyond this there were fine-looking homes that had well-manicured lawns, but farther on there were shanties near a gravel-refining plant. Not far from there was an open pit with torn-up trees along its sides.

Following the road along the lake, to the west of the home, we passed a docking area from which the British were trying out some very large outboard motors. Boats that were propelled by these motors could be heard from far away. There was also a sailboat-rental facility here.

To the south of this area was a small wooden church that I attended only once. I noticed that the priest passed out small, round, white discs to the people who were taking Holy Communion. They looked like plastic discs to me and I wondered how people could swallow them without hurting their throats. I must admit that I was a bit perplexed by the entire service. I do remember that I enjoyed the music, however.

Farther along we came to some large brick buildings that were apparently used as rest homes for the veterans. Beyond these buildings we entered a dense forest. To the west was a small farm. The house had a weakened stone foundation. A little farther along, though, there was a small, white-washed house that had windows that contained round yellow glass. We could tell that it was not occupied. A little farther along we came upon an underground shelter that was still occupied by some men. Our elders permitted us to enter this shelter during one of our treks. They seemed to know the men who lived there. (They may have been Latvians.)

There was a slight flood during the spring thaw of that year and a portion of the playground was flooded. During the flood we saw a man swimming in the mucky water near the playground. He was doing the breast stroke and spitting out water on alternate movements of his head and arms. This was a very unusual and surprising site for us to see.

Our playground had a couple of swings and a May pole-type carousel with long ropes. One little girl who liked the swing very much had a major speech impediment, and she was unable to articulate any intelligible words. This must have been very frustrating for her and it certainly was for those of us who tried to understand her and communicate with her. I was thankful when she was eventually sent to Sweden for speech therapy.

Near the home was a small cement court on which we danced during the fall Līgo festival. Our festivities were not private, though, for many neighbors came to observe us. It was quite a festival indeed. There were oak wreaths and floral headpieces. The adults who were present enjoyed drinking beer—a very popular drink in Germany. I enjoyed dancing and making merry with my friends.

In the medical center on the third floor, children with small warts on their bodies had them removed. The nurses would cut the warts off their bodies. It was thought that this procedure would stop further growths, but I'm not sure if it actually did.

Once, while doing chin-ups from the upper bar of my bunk bed, I slipped and split my jaw open. The injury bled profusely, and I began to think I might bleed to death! The nurse, however, assured me that the wound was not that serious. She patched me up and it healed relatively quickly. (The scar is still there and serves as a reminder to me to be more careful.)

Our shower room was in the basement and we enjoyed going there, especially when the water was good and warm.

Our classes included studying the alphabet and grammar. We also studied elementary arithmetic, reading, and writing. The instructors would read several folktales to us, and so we became familiar with a good many of them, most of which were written by the Grimm Brothers.

The playroom contained such things as toy trucks, rope hoops, large balls, simple games, and other activities. We would pound on tambourines as we danced around in a circle and sang various songs, such as "*Seši Mazi Bundzinieki*" ("Six Little Drummers"). Another one I enjoyed was "*Kur Tu Teci, Kur Tu Teci, Gailīti Man*" ("Where Are You Running, Where Are You Running, Rooster, My Dear?").

It was very pleasant to hear the children singing. We were having a most enjoyable time.

My favorite song was "*Kas Dārza, Kas Dārza?*" These words are roughly translated as "What's in the Garden? What's in the Garden?" Some of the children would remain standing stationary as we sang this ditty, and they represented the trees of the garden. The other children would take turns walking between the "trees." It was great fun for all of us.

Several times we were taken by truck to swimming areas in the vicinity of the home. We would sometimes go to the shore of the Baltic Sea. Most of the time, however, we would go to the weedy and snake-infested lakeshore areas. One of these latter sites was at the outskirts of a city that was busy with traffic and pedestrians. While we were there we went to a park, and there were a number of strangers camping there.

We set up our camp with a number of small tents, did some primitive cooking, and greatly enjoyed swimming in the lake. The sight of a snake swimming in the water frightened me, however, so I decided not to go too far into the weeds because I always worried about what might be lurking there.

In the distance I saw what looked like the tall mast of a vessel, but when we passed that area later I noticed it was not a boat at all. Rather, it was a tall structure that was fastened by cables to the ground. I learned that it was a radio tower. Only later did I understand its function. We were in Rohlsdorf and I heard, "*Kur Tu Teci, Kur Tu Teci, Gailīti Man*" on the radio. As you know, this was one of my favorite songs, so it was thrilling to hear it. The many excursions we took to swimming spots did a great deal to boost our morale and lift our spirits, and I'm sure the exercise was good for us.

Before we moved out of the Malente building, its floors were being ripped up in the hallways so new electrical installations and pipes could be put down. Other improvements were taking place, as well. I learned that the building was going to be a hotel, as it had been originally. It had been built to accommodate persons who were seeking a health resort. This was known as a *kurhaus*, and these were very popular in Germany at that time.

During our stay in Malente, I sometimes noticed women opening bottles of beer and squirting them at each other in a playful manner. They drank from the bottles in our presence. It seemed strange to me to see women drinking, but we got used to it, for balls and parties were greatly enjoyed by our elders.

Most of our outer clothing was handmade from cloth that had been given to us at Sierksdorf. This was necessary because we had lost almost everything at Rügen. We were all well cared for by our stewards. The head of our home was a highly intelligent, gray-haired lady who was fluent in several languages. She was of great value to British intelligence. Her name was Helena Celms.

The British were very kind and generous toward us, and I shall always remember them for their kindnesses. They provided good transportation for us, and I remember us singing songs as we rode to various places in their well-maintained trucks and ambulances.

Our time at Malente had come to a close and we were moved to a large home in Fissau for a couple of weeks. I don't have any specific memories of this place. From here the children were divided into three groups. The children who were ready for adoption were sent to Klingenberg and the others were divided between Müssen and Rohlsdorf. I went to Müssen in the late fall of 1946. Eventually I joined the Klingenberg group, and my brother remained at Müssen. I was later transferred to Rohlsdorf. This was likely because I had been advanced to a higher grade for which there was a teacher. Most likely this teacher was Bernards Austrums. We subsequently went to Klingenberg.

Fissau, Germany

Klingenberg, Germany, fall of 1948

Though I did not get to know any of the children very well, it was somewhat sad to experience these changes. As children were being adopted by Swedish and other couples, we learned about the fine toys they received, such as bicycles. We longed to be adopted ourselves as we dreamed of freedom, mountains of toys, bicycles, and exciting times. My brother and I would likely be adopted together, and the idea of adopting two children at once may not have been all that attractive to would-be adoptive parents.

Realizing that it might be possible for us to be adopted separately, my brother and I competed with each other to be the first selected, even if it would mean that we would be separated from each other. Fortunately, we were adopted at a relatively older age by older parents. My adoptive mother was in her late thirties, and my adoptive father was in his forties, and they were advised to adopt older children due to their older ages.

Personal Reflections

Early on I learned that change is a part of life, and that I need to be open to changes when they come, though I did not particularly like them. To be moved out of one's comfort zone may be good, in that it shows us that our security must be found in something (or someone) other than our current surroundings. This lesson was taught to me over and over again.

In some ways it is strange how one tends to forget the routine things of life, such as eating, sleeping, studying, moving, and meeting people. However, special things that are unexpected and joyful clearly stick out in our memories.

I have learned that most joyful memories relate to joyful relationships with others, especially in early childhood. As we grow, though, our concerns and interests shift. We become less self-centered and begin to look at others and how we relate to them and to God.

As I reflect on those early years, I realize that my awareness of Christian identity grew during my time in Müssen and later in Rohlsdorf. It slowed down a bit during my time in Klingenberg and remained somewhat dormant during my remaining time in Germany.

It was not until I moved to America a few years later when it began to blossom out again. This was particularly true when I worked with young people several years later at the Metigoshe Scout Reservation in Bottineau, North Dakota, and it continued to grow steadily thereafter.

Jesus said, "These things I have spoken to you, that My joy may remain in you, and that your joy may be full. This is My commandment, that you love one another as I have loved you. Greater love has no one than this, than to lay down one's life for his friends. You are My friends if you do whatever I command you... You did not choose Me, but I chose you and appointed you that you should go and bear fruit, and that your fruit should remain, that whatever you ask the Father in My name he may give you".

(JOHN 15:11–16, NKJV)

CHAPTER 5

Müssen and Rohlsdorf

*Now faith is the substance of things hoped for,
the evidence of things not seen.*
(Hebrews 11:1, NKJV)

In this chapter you will learn how we adjusted to new homes both in Müssen and Rohlsdorf. Several people took responsibility for our lives during this era, and I have attempted to describe each one as fully as I remember them. These folk were wonderful examples to each of us, as you will see.

In Rohlsdorf I had my first encounter with Jesus Christ in the person of an English lady named Mrs. Kathleen Yeats, wife of a British man who was in charge of the Save the Children Organization. She was originally on the staff at Malente. She made several visits to us at Rohlsdorf from England. When she would go back to the British Isles, she would send us Bible-oriented pictures to paste into our albums.

What distinguished her, at least to me, was that she placed our needs and interests above her own and bonded with us, and by Christ's love, she caused us kids to bond with each other. This created a concept of family to develop among us, combined with singing and joyful melodies. This was in contrast to the more authoritarian approach of the regular staff members.

Before this deeper insight into Christ's love and experience with relationships, I regarded Jesus as a little genie or good-luck charm. I thought I could hide him in my pocket and pronounce some magic words to summon him to rescue me and instantly fulfill all my wishes. Being in Christ is being in a right relationship of love and joy with one another, not a private fantasy. But understanding this would not come until years later.

Since Kathleen was not with us on a regular basis and did not have to deal with disciplinary matters, she became more popular than the other adult leaders among the children. She was a wonderful witness to Christ by teaching Sunday school lessons to us and leading us in hymn sings while she played the piano. We loved her, and because of her, I eventually became aware of the meaning and possibility of Christian identity.

It may have been because she was so popular among the children that her return visits to the home were limited. But the Christ-love image she implanted within us, through Christ, remained alive.

Our counselors and leaders played such an important role in our lives, both physical and spiritual. They showed us what life is all about and how to be of service to others. I cannot say enough about each of these role models and what I learned from them.

The Müssen Home

Müssen is a municipality in the district of Lauenburg in Schleswig-Holstein. Its name translates literally as "mosses" or "marsh."

Our new home had been the plush residence of a German land baron. In all probability he had several such places under his command. They were small farming centers, and few could be found on general maps and only a few business centers were associated with these places.

Müssen children's home, former manor, landlord mansion/estate

Müssen, Germany

Müssen, Germany, Tolja sitting on left, front slab

As we entered the home, we noticed a large ballroom that was furnished with a fine carpet. A magnificent chandelier hung from the ceiling, and there was a large wall mirror on the right. Then we noticed a winding stairway that led to the second floor. It was quite a place, and I still have vivid memories of its grandeur.

Our new eating place was to the right of the ballroom, and it was quite crowded. The bedrooms for the children were on the second floor, and the counselors' quarters were mostly on the third floor. There was a tower that rose above the main floors, but I never had the opportunity to climb it. My brother, however, had gone up there and he said that it commanded a good view of the countryside.

It was autumn when we arrived in Müssen and the grain was being harvested. We took several walks that gave us many opportunities to observe the countryside. To the right of the home was a huge hedge that separated the property from the main road.

There were wild strawberry plants under a big apple tree, and there was a small garden on the property. There were farm buildings of various sizes and shapes nearby, as well; many of these had the appearance of peasant-type buildings. We would often see horses pulling wagons of hay from the fields. As children, we stayed away from these areas, partly because there was a language barrier between us and the people who lived there.

Sunflowers lifted their lofty heads above the garden where potato plants were seen in abundance. I loved the scarecrows the farmers had placed in the garden in order to frighten the birds away. As we walked along there, we came to a spot where there was a forest on one side and a cow pasture on the other. Then we came to a small stream that ran through a slight ravine. The ground was soggy and dung-covered, and a raging bull came chasing after us but fortunately stopped when it came in front of us. We had invaded his territory and we were quite defenseless should he have decided to attack us. We were very fortunate, indeed, when we saw him turn in the opposite direction. The stream provided us with a shortcut to Rohlsdorf, which was only a couple of kilometers away. Had we stayed on the road, it might have been twice as far.

Once we were stationed in Rohlsdorf we joined with the kids from Müssen to pick our fill of raspberries in some of the same locations I've just mentioned. As you can imagine, the walks we took became much more challenging as fall turned to winter.

A Dedicated and Committed Counselor

When we stayed at Müssen we greatly enjoyed the guidance and help we received from a very dedicated and committed gentleman: our counselor. I regret to say that I do not recall his name, but I certainly do recall his wonderful example to us.

He was like our scoutmaster when we took walks away from the home. During the wintertime he would build a large fire on the lawn of our home. He showed us how to gather kindling and wood for the fires. Most of what we brought to him was in the form of rotten wood and dead branches, which worked well once the fire was blazing.

Snow turned the region into a beautiful winter wonderland. We would take our sleds with us when we went hiking. The counselor I just mentioned took us to a place we had never visited before. It was quite a journey through the snow. We crossed a field and then we went onto a large expanse of ice that covered a long and narrow lake, which may have actually been just a widening in the river.

There were fractures on the surface of the ice, but it appeared to be about one foot thick. It was a strange and wonderful experience for us to be able to "walk on water," as we had heard Jesus did when he was on Earth. Much later, when we were at Rohlsdorf, we learned that someone had invented large, buoyant shoes with which a person could actually walk on water! We found this a bit hard to believe. Regrettably, I never had the opportunity to try them out. I found it interesting to notice the bubbles of various sizes and shapes that one could see beneath the surface of the ice.

We were eventually sent to the Rohlsdorf Home, and the children and adults who were there came out to greet us warmly. Rohlsdorf is a village in the Prignitz district of Germany. It is a seaside community. Near the home I spotted a partly submerged motorboat not far from the shore. My curiosity got the best of me, so I climbed into the boat and knocked loose a small copper wire coil that I found in one of the gauges. This gave me a slight feeling of guilt, but it was a part of my nature to explore such things. My insatiable desire to know how things work compelled me to explore everything I could.

Unfortunately, my brother and I did not get along well in Müssen due to a hostile, competitive spirit we both shared. Perhaps I was a bit jealous of him, because he was rated as the best student and he was well-liked by all the counselors. Tolja managed to get close to the young son of one of the helpers (Mrs. Purins), and this enabled him to play with many fine toys, such as trucks and airplanes.

After I moved to Rohlsdorf and my brother stayed at Müssen, we found that our affection for each other grew, thereby proving the old adage, "Absence makes the heart grow fonder." This held true throughout our lives, even after we came to the States. As adults we once again found that we enjoyed each other's company, especially after we were both married and had families. We greatly enjoyed each other's company during those years and our spouses and children interacted whenever we came together.

We corresponded with each other on a regular basis despite our differences, and I even got to speak to him by phone at least once while I was at Rohlsdorf. We also had a good number of opportunities to get together, because Müssen and Rohlsdorf were not that far apart.

Though I had little formal schooling while I was in Müssen, I became quite a student in Rohlsdorf. I believe it was March of 1947 when I arrived there, so spring was just around the corner.

Rohlsdorf, Germany

A Whole New Era in My Life

At the Rohlsdorf home I began to experience a whole new era in my life. It was here where I met a number of kind counselors. They taught me so much. I've already mentioned Miss Rozīte Briedis, who became Mrs. Rose Austrums. She was a chief and lasting influence in my life and the lives of the other children. This good woman had been with us since we were at Majori.

In Rohlsdorf her chief assignment seemed to be the maintenance and supervision of the library. She also taught literature and Latvian folk songs. She was the instructor of the children who were in kindergarten, as well, so as you can imagine, she was a very busy person. She was quite dedicated to her jobs and to the children with whom she worked.

She often accompanied us on our hikes and outings and was usually present at all home functions in which the children participated. Quite early in my stay here I visited the library and read several books, including fairy tales and folktales. Often, Rose would read these stories to us as a group, and I always enjoyed the animated way with which she read.

Rose selected me and Mika (aka Stanislaus Mikaskins) to be a part of a special reading group. Unfortunately, Mika and I did not get along well together. He was much taller than me and I remember a conspicuous scar on his right cheek, which caused facial deformities that distorted the position of his mouth. This had turned him into a defensive and self-conscious bully. Even so, he would sometimes make me laugh out loud, even to the point of uncontrolled giggling. This would sometimes happen as we sat together before Rose started reading, and I'm sure she was not pleased by this, though she never showed anger or displeasure outwardly. I soon realized that I might be offending Rose by this behavior and I knew it was inappropriate, so I began to work on changing it. However, for many years afterward, under situations of stress and formality, I would continue to burst out with laughter even though it was probably seen as being inappropriate for me to do so. There were times when I actually laughed so hard that I would wet my pants!

Actually, I frequently had to run whenever I had "to go" very urgently, and I was unable to "hold it" for very long. Had I simply gotten up and made a run for it during every such impulse, I would have been the subject of talk and ridicule for all. I lived with this inner torment for many years. Finally, I discovered a way to deal with such moments, and this helped me, of course, to appreciate what other children with similar issues were going through.

As adults, we need to remember that harsh and threatening words will aggravate and worsen such situations, and sometimes precipitate the very reactions they seek to avoid. It then becomes a self-fulfilling prophecy. Such reactions are typical when a child is being physically or emotionally abused. There is a huge difference between discipline that is administered in a Christ-governed way and punitive, accusative yelling at a child.

I remember Rose reading to us the story of *The Ugly Duckling* by Hans Christian Andersen. Sometimes I felt like the duckling that grew into a beautiful swan, and I hoped that the same thing might happen to me. Another story she read to us was *The Adventures of Tom Sawyer* by Mark Twain. I could relate to so many of the episodes in this story, particularly those that related to Tom's and Huck's mischiefs. Certainly I was quite adventurous myself.

I don't know the title or author of one story she read to us, but I sure do remember its contents. It was about a truant lad who had to be taken to a reform school where he managed to get even with a bully who was bigger than himself. The story showed how the boy acquired a measure of self-discipline. I was so fascinated to learn that he went on to become an airplane pilot.

From Rose we also learned a good number of folk songs, and she also taught us games and folk dancing, which I greatly enjoyed. She instilled within us a deep appreciation for Latvian literature and music, including the grand old hymns of the Church. One of my favorite church songs was "*Pie Rokas Nem Un Vadi*," which is translated as "O Take My Hand, Dear Father." Other more familiar hymns that we learned were "A Great and Mighty Wonder," "A Mighty Fortress Is Our God," "Ah, Holy Jesus," "From Heaven Above," and "O Come, O Come, Immanuel" (which we sang to the tune of Dmitri Bortnianski's "St. Petersburg"). Others included "Praise Ye the Father for His Loving Kindness," "Silent Night, Holy Night," "O How a Rose E'er Blooming," and "O Sacred Head Now Wounded."

We also learned the Latvian national anthem, "*Dievs, Sveti Latviju*," which is translated as "God Bless Latvia." Learning to sing all these hymns, carols, and anthems filled me with a sense of wonder and joy, and I developed a love of singing and my love of my homeland grew.

Műssen, Germany, Volodja front on left, 1948, 30th anniversary of
Latvia's Independence, children's choir from Rohlsdorf, Germany

The home had a large ballroom with a piano, which I learned to plunk
on, a single key at a time. I soon learned to play some simple tunes. One
song was "Marlene." I remember German soldiers marching and singing
this song. Sometimes they would be accompanied by an accordion. This
song could also be heard on the radio.

I appreciate all that Rose did to preserve in me a sense of continuity
and identity. After I moved to the United States in March 1949, I got to
see her again. She had been hired as a maid by a family in Fargo, North
Dakota. Not long thereafter she married Mr. Austrums and moved to
Omaha, Nebraska. Through her I was able to reestablish contact with
some of the children of our group as well as counselors who had helped
us all along the way.

Rose possessed an enthusiastic youthfulness and vitality throughout
the time we were together in spite of all the challenges and changes we
experienced. In truth, however, I did not really get to know her personally
until we had all settled in the United States.

Our Counselors and Teachers

Another one of our helpers was Mr. Arnolds Zvēriņš, who appeared to be the head of the education aspect of our home. He had originally been a journalist in Latvia. He had received his early schooling in both Russia and France, and his higher education at the University of Moscow. What an interesting man he was, though I did not get to know him very well due to the fact that his main responsibility was in the field of administration rather than teaching.

I do remember once when he gave me a prize for being the top student in the home. It was a wooden, ever-sharp pencil, plus a box of water colors. The fact that I received such an honor at such a young age did wonders for me and propelled me for greater success in the future.

Unfortunately, while sick in bed, curiosity got the better of me and I took the pencil apart. The spring popped out and flew out of sight. The pencil worked no more. I felt very bad about this, and was troubled for a long time afterward due to the guilt I felt.

I respected Mr. Zvēriņš very much. His wife, Mrs. Zvēriņš, served as an administrator. I didn't get to know her very well, either, but I do remember how she would distribute candy to us from her office on the second floor. Since the German mark and lower denominations of currency had become obsolete, we were given batches of the older currency as an "allowance," which we could use to "purchase" candy, such as chocolate buttons and Hershey M&M's along with British chocolate candies of various sorts. We could use it, also, to purchase Beech-Nut chewing gum.

Arnolds and Veronika Zvēriņš, 1957, USA

Arnolds Zvēriņš

Marta Bulova (*Martas Kundze*) was my "foster mother." I remembered her from Malente as a very industrious, concerned, affectionate, and non-temperamental woman. She made our dress pants and knitted our fancy sweaters. She also knitted our swimsuits and other garments. When we would take walks in the winter she would wear a fur coat that had seen better days. Nonetheless, I loved to touch it and feel its softness. This caused me to call her "Kitten," and she seemed to love my using this term of affection.

When the other boys' counselor, Miss Krēsliņš, heard about this nickname that I had given to Marta, she rebuked me. I guess she felt that the name "Kitten" was disrespectful to Mrs. Bulova, but I did not mean it to be. Miss Krēsliņš always seemed to be unnecessarily harsh with the children in our group, and she would take our toys away, especially if she felt that we had hurt or abused one of her boys.

It seemed to me that all the boys in Miss Krēsliņš' group were bullies. There were some in our own group who were bullies, as well, such as one I've already mentioned—Mika, who would kick others when he was angry. I remember one time when he spat into my soup. Since I knew the counselors wouldn't listen to my complaints, I spat into his soup, too.

That was a mistake, though, for my action caused another boy, Alberts, who always wanted to be "the head of the show," to try to dominate me. I knew that my spitting was asking for trouble from him, though I don't recall that he ever took revenge on me for that act, except for continuing to boss me around.

Some of the Other Children at Rohlsdorf

One of my closest friends at the time was Ivans Drozdovs, a blond-haired boy whose tuberculosis caused him to have to remain behind when the rest of us left Germany. He and I shared so many of the same traits and we both had tuberculosis, but his condition must have been worse than mine. Because of our disease we would be asked to leave the table in the evenings so we could take baths and get sufficient sleep. I remember him showing me how one's leg vibrates with rapid muscular rhythm when the foot is raised and rests firmly against an object.

One of the cuter children in our group was little Nikolajs Kalpinovs, whom we called "Niki." He would at times take the role of "nasty baby" while the rest of us would chase after him as his "punishing mother or father." He could do at least one thing I could not do, which was that he could whistle with his tongue folded between his lips, a skill I never really acquired.

One of the boys was a half-Gypsy named Jānis Seskovs. We called him "Jancis." I regarded him as a bully, especially at nights in our bedroom. One night he began crying out as if he was in pain, and I felt a little sorry for him. Marta and some others thought he was just trying to attract attention. This was not the case, for radiographs revealed that one of his toes was broken.

Radiographs and medical procedures were performed at the Lübeck Barracks Hospital. This was where we went for regular checkups. Children with mumps would stay there until they recovered.

Two of our boys had to leave for Sweden, and this brought sadness to all of us, for this meant that a part of our family was leaving. Marta wept, and so did Mrs. Anna Birze, who took these boys onto her lap, hugged them, and recounted some precious memories she had of them. These two boys left in early 1948.

Another boy, Jurijs Sergukovs, was the son of a Russian secret police agent, but he had been placed in the Majore home while he was quite young, so that he was very much a Latvian in every way. He was taken to Russia at around the same time as the two boys I just mentioned were taken to Sweden.

Around this same time at Rohlsdorf I remember when a couple of military officers in long trench coats and flat-top hats, whom we assumed to be Russians, entered our bedroom to identify children they desired to reclaim. Their presence frightened us quite a lot, and Vija Ceriņš cried furiously at the thought of having her sister, Gunta, taken to Russia. Fortunately she was not taken. I, too, was concerned because my brother and I had Russian-sounding names.

I acquired some privileges by befriending Juris Krauklis, who lived with his parents on the third floor of our building. I often visited his upstairs playroom and played with his lead soldiers, miniature cannons, and military vehicles. I was certainly impressed by the number of toys he had. His model factories and shops that had been made by Germans were most enjoyable to me. These models had lathes and human figures that were moved by spring motors that were concealed under the floors of these structures. As I understand it, these miniatures had been left in the attic of our building by some Polish children who had occupied the premises before we did.

As usual, however, it was not long before my friend and I had torn into these models to see how they worked and thereby ruined them. When one of the counselors learned about this, she rebuked us by saying that we were very destructive children.

Juris also had the privilege of being taken into a city once in a while. On one of these occasions he was able to purchase sets of postage stamps that were collectibles, and he gave me a sheet of these stamps. This began my stamp collection, which includes Latvian, Russian, and German stamps. One day I happened to see an envelope with a stamp that was marked "USA" on it. I thought the country was pronounced "Usa" (Oosa). We also found some USA stamps in the attic.

I really liked Juris and his kindness to me. He was a bit self-conscious due to his being somewhat chubby, taller than me, and not really a part of our group. He never participated in any of our group activities. When I visited with him just before I departed for Hamburg, he showed off his newborn baby brother to me. He was very proud of him.

There was another Juris whom I got to know. He was calm, reserved, and intelligent, and all the counselors seemed to love him.

Two of Our Teachers

Our main instructor was Mr. Austrums. We regarded him as being harsh and even sometimes cruel. He never hesitated to shout, pull our hair and ears, whack us with a birch branch, and even slap children in the face whenever he perceived us as being unruly or disobedient. Nonetheless, he was a good teacher, and from him I learned many of the Old Testament stories about Daniel in the lions' den, Samson and Delilah, David and Goliath, Noah's ark, Moses and the Ten Commandments, the plagues, the Exodus, and the story of Adam and Eve.

Under his direction we memorized portions of the Gospel of John. (I still own a copy of the Gospel of John in Latvian.) He also taught proper grammar to us and we learned a great deal about Latvian history. In addition, we learned some elementary math and arithmetic. I did well enough in math to be advanced to a more difficult mathematics course, which was taught by Mr. Kuzmiņš. I struggled in this course somewhat, especially with the mathematical problems that were put forth in our textbook, *Matematika* by Karlis Kaufmanis. I was particularly perplexed by the verbal problems that were presented in that textbook.

I persevered, however, and managed to master most of the material. This resulted in my being presented with the best-student prize in the spring of 1948. This was a wonderful surprise to me!

For a while we learned some things from men in the woodshop, but this was discontinued after we broke too many hacksaw blades.

During one of Mr. Austrums' classes I was sitting next to Mika on a bench. He was chewing on some candy and making loud, slurping noises. This was very distracting and disgusting to me, and I could not concentrate on my studies because of it. I even became quite nauseated. To this day I really have a hard time tolerating such sounds when others are eating.

Mr. Austrums' face always bled after he shaved, and his jaw and face were filled with swollen pimples. He attributed his skin problems to diseases he had had when he was younger. When he came to America, though, these problems were treated with success. Also, his sour nature sweetened, and he seemed kinder and less stressed. He had been born in the Latvian town of Vilaka, which is located in the province of Latgale. He attended high school in Balvi and went to a two-year teachers' college in

Rezekens, but his actual teacher's training had begun in secondary school. This was the pattern of schooling in Latvia. He became a principal of elementary schools in Latvia and then became a sergeant in the German army.

My math teacher, Mr. Kuzmiņš, had been a policeman in Latvia. He was quite a bit kinder and more easygoing than Mr. Austrums. I never developed a close relationship with either of these men, but I did learn a lot from them.

Mr. Kuzmiņš had a collection of magazines that were similar to *Life* magazine. I had the opportunity to look through some of these and found quite a number of photos of gruesome war scenes.

Other Helpers

Our main nurse was named Anna, and her small medicine room was on the second floor of our building. She would give us inoculations and treat our cuts and bruises. It seemed that I always had open sores on my knees. Once, when I went to her office complaining of a sore stomach, she put me on a cot near the door and massaged my lower abdomen. This brought great relief to me.

On another occasion I had fallen off a swing while standing on it. I believe that either the board seat had broken or the chains had gotten disengaged from it. At any rate, I landed on the ground headfirst. This had knocked me out, and the next thing I knew I was standing in Anna's office. She was treating me for a large open cut under my jaw and a bleeding tooth mark on the inside of my mouth.

There were two small "sick rooms" near her office. Once, when I had the flu, I shared one of these rooms with Vija, who was quite sick and had to use the "potty" in the room over and over again. One of my friends was in the other "sick room," and he asked me to visit him, which I gladly did. However, Marta severely rebuked me for this. This caused me to go back to my bed and withdraw myself under the covers. She then proceeded to scold me for trying to suffocate myself!

While I was in the sick room I was so happy when the head nurse brought me an extra treat with a meal—sliced oranges! None of the other children were so fortunate. Apparently, I must have been one of her favorites, and I remember her as a very understanding person who was admired and respected by the children.

Jack Richards was the British head of the home. I never really got to know him, but I realized that it was because of him that the home was provided for and the workers were paid. He was also in charge of the vehicles, which were stored in a concrete lot. I accompanied him to the parking lot one day, and while he was talking to the mechanic in the garage, I climbed into a small, green Volkswagen, which appeared to be a wreck but was actually being restored. I picked up a bolt out of a can on the floor inside of the car and for some inexplicable reason I used it to smash out one of the dashboard meters. After the mechanic discovered what had happened, he came to the home and threatened to break my neck!

Mr. Richards on left and Mrs. Richards second from right

The elders, however, warned him not to do anything to me. They explained that Mr. Richards may have taken an undue risk in bringing me along. Thankfully, I was spared any actual punishment, but my sense of guilt was aroused and that was my "spanking." In many ways guilt had become my teacher.

Antons was a Lithuanian man who served as custodian and all-around handyman. He had a fold-up camera. He often took photos and many of these had his image in them. He was able to do this by climbing on someone's back or doing other stunts while the camera whirred away. We often saw him chopping wood outside or feeding the coal furnace in the basement. He was always friendly with the youngsters, but due to the language barrier, real communication with him was lacking.

Rohlsdorf, Germany, likely summer 1947, photo snapped by Antons, the groundskeeper, with his camera set on chair, delayed action/self-timer

There were red-bellied lizards in our area and I remember one time when Antons picked one up and told us that one bite of this lizard could kill him. This really fed our fears. On another occasion he managed to acquire the use of a fishing boat and pulled us along in another boat in the lake behind the home. This was a very exciting experience for us.

Antons left the home just before I did, and Marta had to go to the hospital for an abdominal surgery. Upon her return, she had to lie in a bathtub full of water as a part of her therapy. The health of Jack Richards also began to fail, and he returned to England. It is he who invited some of the children to have fellowship with British people in the home. I remember one such occasion when I drank tea (with cream and sugar) and ate biscuits, British-style. I was told that I should feel honored by this privilege, because it enabled me to "observe proper manners and etiquette."

Learning about Jesus

The home made some attempts to have Latvian pastors come on Sundays. I remember one of these pastors who showed us a Latvian castle/fortress, which was surrounded by a moat. He used this to illustrate his teaching about Luther's hymn, "A Mighty Fortress Is Our God." Other pastors came from time to time, but we did not have services on many Sundays.

There were a few Sundays when we were taken to churches in the surrounding area. Some of these were quite formal, with elevated pulpits and closed-in pews. I remember one of these churches in particular. It was located in a nearby city and we visited it twice. It had an adjoining cemetery in which I saw beautiful flowers adorning the graves. In the entryway of the church was a marble baptismal font.

Children from Rohlsdorf and Müssen with counselors/elders after church

In another church that we attended I heard a memorable sermon about the Good Samaritan. As the pastor preached, I noticed a stained-glass window that showed the story most vividly. We also visited a country church that was not far away. The sides of the church building were covered with lush, green ivy and it had the most beautiful flower gardens I had ever seen. It was in connection with a burial that took place in this cemetery that we were reminded of the death of Latvia's president, Karlis Ulmanis, who we were told had stood up for Latvia's independence before crowds of sneering people who had been duped by the Russians.

I remember that we had been taught that thunderstorms were the result of God driving His chariot over us to execute His wrath and judgment. I remember during some of these storms that I tried to trace the course of His chariot by listening for the direction of the thunder! I must admit that I was scared, though.

Once, a professional photographer came to our home. He called some of our children who were playing in the front yard to gather in front of a large, clay flowerpot. I saw what was taking place from an upper floor of the home and raced down the stairs to be included in the photo, but I was too late! The photo was taken without me. I'm sure it would have been one of the better photos of me!

I remember one terrifying time during a storm when Miss Krēsliņš warned that if the children did not behave, God would descend through the ceiling and punish them with birch branches. This caused us to clam up immediately!

Singing hymns during worship services instilled within us a sense of beauty and wonder, but Jesus himself did not mean much to me personally—yet. It seemed to me that Jesus was an invisible, ghostly, ever-present brother whom I could command at will. However, there was nothing living or personal about Him.

In Mrs. Kathleen Yeats (whom I mentioned before), though, I sensed something different and unique. Her personal warmth was kindled by something that seemed very holy indeed. My encounter with her in Sunday school classes and other situations planted the seeds that remained dormant until I arrived in the States. Under the influence of my pastor-father and other Christ-governed individuals, this seed eventually burst forth in full blossom.

Mrs. Yeats, outdoor sports

Personal Reflections

I thank God for Mrs. Yeats! When she was unable to rejoin us in person, she sent us little pictures of Bible personalities to paste into our albums. She had been at Klingenberg with her husband, a British officer with the Save the Children Organization but moved to England. From her I learned a lot about Christian fellowship, worship, service, outreach, witnessing, and joy. She planted many precious seeds within us, and these seeds grew to fruition in my life later on, after we were transported to the United States.

The apostle John wrote, "He was in the world, and the world was made through Him, and the world did not know Him. He came to His own, and His own did not receive Him. But as many as received Him, to them He gave the right to become children of God, to those who believe in His name: who were born, not of blood, nor of the will of the flesh, nor of the will of man, but of God. And the Word became flesh and dwelt among us, and we beheld His glory, the glory as of the only begotten of the Father, full of grace and truth".

(JOHN 1:10–14, NKJV)

I began to grow more and more curious about Him, and I am so thankful that He (through Christ-governed people) found me when I was seeking Him. He surely is "the way, the truth, and the life" and no one can go unto the Father unless they do so through Him. (See John 14:6.)

CHAPTER 6

SPECIAL OUTINGS
AND EVENTS

Eye has not seen, nor ear heard, nor have entered into the heart
of man the things which God has prepared for those who love Him.
(1 CORINTHIANS 2:9, NKJV)

As I felt more comfortable about getting to know people, my confidence in myself began to grow. I learned that people are like tiny pixels of color within a much-larger picture. The more people we meet and get to know, the more focused and clear the image of Jesus Christ becomes within us.

My curiosity about Jesus was like a jigsaw puzzle with many pieces, and this puzzle developed little by little as I grew. I learned much later on that love for and knowledge of Christ came through live bonding with Christ-governed people, such as Mrs. Yeats. This came well before I received wisdom and inspiration from the Holy Scriptures, such as we see in the verse above.

We can easily become addicted to ideas, ideologies, philosophies, and even the scriptures without actually linking up with Jesus. When this happens our god becomes Me, Myself, and I. Remember, Satan knows the

Scriptures well, even by heart, and this enabled him to tempt Jesus in the wilderness. Judas probably knew the Scriptures well, also.

May the true Spirit of Christ resonate throughout the pages of this book, and may you come to know Him personally if you do not know Him now. You will discover that Christ—His way and His love—are everything to you.

The Building Was on Fire!

During one of our noon naps in 1947 or 1948, we were awakened by a great commotion outside. When we looked out the window we saw a massive column of smoke that was coming from the apartment building where most of our counselors and teachers stayed. Their building was on fire!

As a precaution, we were rushed outside, and we saw that furniture and other belongings had been removed from the burning building. It took a while for the firemen to arrive. The first fire-emergency vehicle had a large wheel with hoses and a hand-operated pump; it was situated on two large wooden wheels. Except for the hose, this vehicle didn't help much.

A trailer-type engine was later brought over and it was parked near the southwestern side of the building, near the lake. This enabled the firemen to pump water directly from the lake. Thanks to their efforts, the entire building did not burn completely down, as one might have thought it would. However, much of the upper, western portion was destroyed. The rooms in that section had been completely gutted and ruined, and there was a strong odor of charred and rotting wood that permeated the building for months afterward.

Hikes and Treks throughout the Surrounding Area

This section provides a more in-depth look at some of the walks we took. As you know, we took many hikes throughout the year, and to me each one was an exploration that was full of discoveries. I have blended some of these walks together in the following paragraphs.

Not far from the home was a small complex of farm buildings, including a large barn. There was a small bullpen there and we would occasionally see a large bull that had a ring through his nose. It would snort and kick, and the children would be so excited that they would tease the bull in order to see it act up more. The owner warned us to get away.

It was interesting to see the sheep getting sheared in the barn. The wool would be removed with electric clippers, while a German shepherd kept us at a distance. We noted a large stork's nest on the roof of the barn. In light of the stories we had heard about storks bringing babies, we would study these birds. We discovered how they gave birth to their own young annually, but I never saw one of them carry a human infant with its beak!

Not far away from the barn, we saw a porch with tobacco drying on lines and several old men were standing idly by and smoking away. There was a repair shop to the west of the barn. I noticed the hull of an old motorboat in there. It looked like they were trying to rebuild it. I believe this was the same boat I had seen lying in the water to the south of our home. It must have been pulled on shore by a truck.

I remembered how I had forcefully knocked off one or two of the components of the engine with a gear or shaft I had found in the boat when it was on the bank. This was not an attempt at vandalism, but an honest effort to try to learn more about the boat's operation. I continued this exploration by trying to crack open one of these components by throwing it against the concrete walkway that led to the building. I felt some guilt because I knew they were trying to recondition this boat, and I wondered how much the damage I had caused had set back their work.

As we continued our journey, we saw some straw-covered peasant huts to the right. I visited one of these homes after I learned that some of the children had been given apples by the people who lived there. The furniture and other accommodations within the home were very primitive. The occupants were nice to me, though, and they gave me a couple of green, brown-spotted apples.

The road continued northward and we saw a cow pasture on the right side and a grain field on the left. We would sometimes hear a tractor working in the fields. A bit farther along we saw large basswood trees on both sides of the road, and some of these had to be cut down after a windstorm blew through.

During the spring thaw the water streamed across the road in rapid torrents. This provided us with an exciting contrast with the bright, melting snow on a sunny day. One day, as we walked though this area, Marta rebuked me for not wearing a hat, because she knew that I was susceptible to earaches from the winter cold.

Once in a while we would see a calf or two with their heads stuck between the wires of the fence. They were cute little creatures, and it seemed that they were able to free themselves as we drew closer. A bit farther along we saw a large garden that was filled with beautiful flowers, and there was a field of rutabagas nearby. During the fall these rutabagas would be piled up along the ditch or in stacks in the fields in preparation for the winter months, when they would be covered with straw.

Rutabagas were a source of food for both animals and humans. We loved to eat them raw. The farmers would permit us to sample them as we went along our way.

In a wooded section to our right, there were chains and rigs that were used to thin out some of the pine trees. We then came to a trail that went southward toward the lake. Along this trail we would use the bushes when nature called.

A paved highway was not far away. It had a cobblestone bridge over a stream. On the other side of the bridge we noticed fishermen laying their nets in the water. (This was just south of our home.) One of the fish that was frequently caught here was known as the *lidaka*, which is something like a northern pike. It was at this point that the Müssen children would sometimes meet us. It was always good to see them. We would join together and walk across the highway and continue along a more primitive road.

This road had some sudden drops, and it led past some peasant homes and huge stacks of firewood. We entered a small community that had a white stucco building that was used as a movie theater. We saw at least two movies here, and one of these concerned a place in Asia where rice was grown. In this motion picture we saw barefooted men working in terraces of water with the help of teams of oxen or water buffalo.

This movie depicted the paganism of the people by revealing their idolatry, superstitions, and sun-worship. At the end of the movie they showed an eclipse of the sun, as if to emphasize that this was a land of spiritual darkness. I thought the movie was weird.

To the west of our building we would take a route that was close to the lake, and usually pass through the alley between the apartment building and a brick wall. We would eventually emerge upon a road that led into a forest. As we did so, we would pass over a smelly stream of sewage that flowed over the road toward the lake. In the summer months we would swim in the lake at this very spot, and we would find broken pieces of glass and pottery in the mud at the bottom. I don't believe this was a healthy experience for us kids!

One time, as we walked along this road, we encountered a cow lying on its side. There was obvious evidence of it having diarrhea. We told one of the people in a nearby house about its condition.

A sawmill was nearby, and stacks of freshly cut lumber were kept there. I remember some of the plant life in this area. There were lilac, pinchberry, and willow bushes there, along with a berry-alder plant that was known as *ieva*. Not far from here there were raspberry bushes that we would duly strip during the berry season.

As we came closer to the lake, some of the children noticed a large snake that was wound around the trunk of a small tree. Mr. Kuzmiņš threw a rock at the snake from a distance and apparently wounded or killed it. After that experience, I always hesitated before going into this area.

One spot that we all enjoyed was a place of freedom for us. It was a wooded area where we were free to run and play without any fear of us damaging anything or being damaged in any way. Badger and mole holes abounded in this area. We picked and ate nuts and mushrooms here.

There was a swamp a few hundred feet away. Men would harvest the reeds and rushes to make thatch for roofs. Now and then we would see a snake, but the children had learned how to stamp them to death. I remember that one of our male counselors once told us that a certain snake was capable of freezing solid during the winter while hiding in a hole or a stump. He said that if we found one we could actually break it into pieces as we would an icicle, and yet it could thaw out and come alive in the spring. This did not sound right to me, and I have never been able to verify this!

Farther westward, near the swamp, we saw a tall ladder leaning against a tree. There was an observation-type structure near the top of the tree. Some theorized that it must be a watchtower to help men keep a lookout for wolves or other animals. It must have been used by hunters in that region.

It was interesting for me to study the various kinds of lichen, fungi, and mosses in this area. I guess I was an amateur mycologist! On another road that was very close by we found horse chestnut trees. We understood that local people would use the nuts to make soaps, so we gathered several to sell to them. We would throw sticks at the prickly clusters of brownish growths. When they fell we would look for the pair of large brown nuts inside.

We had a little garden plot in which we grew potatoes, cucumbers, beans, onions, peas, carrots, and other vegetables. We would help take care of the plot and pick the vegetables. We also had some big, beautiful sunflowers. Farmers in the area had cellars in which they would store vegetables, and they allowed us to store some of our vegetables there, as well.

As we headed westward from our home, along the lake shore, we followed a foot trail past some willows, cranberry bushes, red dogwood bushes, cow parsnips, and other types of vegetation. Several times, Mr. Austrums took us to a spot under a large shade tree for outdoor classes, and often he would let us run around the area. It was all great fun.

We would wade out to a little island in the lake. It was thickly covered with very tall grasses that reached above our heads. We would trample this grass down and make trails. The grass was very sharp, and we would often get cuts as we went through it. In fact, I still have a scar near my right knee that came from one such cut. Many of the trees on this island were dead and gray. The others we climbed until they were nearly dead, as well.

We would pick the white berries of the red dogwood trees and squirt the pits at each other. There seemed to be no limit to what we were able to devise for having fun. Being in nature was a source of great enjoyment for us all, and to be with other children in that environment made it all the more meaningful.

We also made shelters from the tall grass. We only permitted our best friends to enter these. We defended our "forts" by giving due warning to all others. Our imaginations were busy and it was generally a happy time for us.

As we continued eastward, we came to a road that passed through some birch and maple trees. We would sometimes gather birch branches to make brooms. These branches were sometimes used to spank us, as well.

In the summer of 1948, a beach area at the lake became a site for vacationers who would come with their little house trailers and enjoy the water and sun. This changed the whole picture for us, and we had less opportunity to explore and have adventures there.

However, a bit farther along we would enjoy swimming in the lake. Sometimes we even went "skinny dipping," but due to strangers being around the area, we did very little of this. I learned to stay above water that was deeper than my height. Our knitted swimming suits were made of wool, and they would expand and become too large for us. They were quite scratchy, also, and that may be why we would go swimming in the nude from time to time. While we swam, our counselors would lie in the sun on the beach and enjoy some relaxation.

Rohlsdorf, Germany, Baltic Sea beach, Volodja in front to right of girl,
likely summer 1947, Antons, groundskeeper, on top

The lawn of our home was "mowed" by a flock of sheep; they also fertilized it. I remember the spring thaw of 1947, when we found under the melting snow the little white flowers that signaled spring's arrival to us. It was good to see them again. Someone once said, "God gives us the changing seasons to teach us gratitude," and grateful I was to know that spring was just around the corner. The words of Shelley were ringing true: "If winter comes, can spring be far behind?"

To the east of the home, there were a good number of hazelnut bushes. Picking and eating these was a great pastime for us. Once in a while a truck would take us to areas where hazelnut bushes were especially tall and thick, and we would get busy gathering them in bags to take back to the home. These nuts were particularly tasty and I'm sure they were good for us. Trucks would take us to areas for raspberry picking, as well. We would spend hours picking (and eating) these luscious berries.

When a chimney sweep arrived to clean out the smoke stacks atop our building, we thought he must be the devil since he looked so filthy and unkempt. We would sneer at him and call him names, and this would arouse his bitterness toward us.

Life for us in Rohlsdorf was healthy, enjoyable, and fun for the most part. In the next section I will share about some of the events that gave us joy and happiness.

Time outside

Beach

Festivals, Holiday Celebrations, and Other Exciting Events

In the autumn of 1947, we celebrated a wonderful *Līgo Svētki* (festival). For this occasion, we had put four tall posts at the corners of the lawn and then we placed large cans that were filled with oil-soaked rags at the top. Once lighted, these cans burned brightly, and their flames would last almost all-night long. We had made wreaths from oak branches for the ladies who wore their usual costumes. We sang *Līgo* songs and munched on *pīrāgs*, which were made of wiener-type buns and stuffed with chopped ham. The adults drank beer and made merry, and everyone was in a happy mood.

At Christmastime we would paste together chains of paper rings that were to be used as ornaments on the Christmas tree. On Christmas Eve of 1947, I remember taking time to carefully comb my curly hair. As I was taking a look at it in the hallway mirror, one of the women, perhaps Marta, made a comment that I had very beautiful curly hair. This embarrassed me somewhat and caused me to feel a bit shy about my hair's appearance.

The Christmas tree was in the playroom and it was filled with lighted candles—a very beautiful sight to behold. The children sat on the floor in front of the tree and sang Christmas carols. Then we were given our presents—combs, candies, pencils, and balloons. (We had never seen balloons before, so these were very special to us.)

I remember that my balloon was black, while the others had various colors. We would blow them up so big that they would burst. There was nothing particularly Christian about this event, but we did enjoy ourselves. The children from Müssen came to join us with their sleds and skates, but the ice on the lake was too thin for them.

On several different occasions, a truck would come to the home with a movie projector, screen, and various films. I remember one of these that dealt with Indians making canoes out of birch bark. Another film had to do with track-and-field events, and this helped us prepare for our own upcoming Müssen-Rohlsdorf track-and-field day.

A blue-and-orange tinted film (a forerunner of color films that are common today) was about lobster and crab fishing. Another one of these was about "mining" amber from the sea. Other movies we saw dealt with how toys are produced by using a lathe, insect control, various tales (including *Puss in Boots*), etc. These films proved to be both educational and enjoyable for us.

A magician came to our home once, and he gave us a very fascinating and impressive demonstration of his talents. He wore a black suit and top hat. We sat enthralled as he concealed a lighted candle in a closed metal tube, which he then put in the inside pocket of his coat. Then he removed the candle and its flame was still burning! He also did the stereotypical rabbit-out-of-the-hat trick and the many-scarves-from-one-scarf trick.

He brought a clown along with him, and he had the clown balance a piece of white bread on his head. When the magician turned the other way, however, the clown devoured the bread. All the children found this quite amusing, and great peals of laughter filled our playroom. The clown also had a large bottle hidden under his loose-fitting garb. He would take the bottle out from time to time and consume large quantities of the beverage it contained while the magician was not looking. The children would laugh, and the magician would turn around as if to wonder what was going on. He also brought puppets and puppeteers with him, and the puppet show was most enjoyable.

Around the middle of his presentation the magician dared anyone to try him out and see if he was faking. He asked if anyone would like to come forward so he could turn him or her into a mushroom. Rose was sitting next to me and I asked her, "Is he telling the truth? Can he turn us into mushrooms?" She replied, "I'm not sure." Whatever the case, none of us dared to go forward, and the magician continued with his show.

Haircuts, Festive Balls, Track-and-Field Events, and Birthdays

A barber would come to our home to give us haircuts. He would throw a white sheet with a hole in it over our heads. At first, he used manually operated clippers, but when these were worn out from overuse, they would pull our hair and cause us great discomfort. Later on, however, we were happy to see that he brought electric clippers to use on our hair, and these were so much better, even though we could feel their heat and vibrations. He was a very friendly man, and he usually wore a white barber's outfit.

Our playroom was used from time to time for festive balls. These were opportunities for the staff members to have fun in the form of dancing and drinking. We were supposed to be sleeping when these occurred, but sleeping seemed impossible with such merry-making going on.

To prepare for these festivities, Antons would spruce up the room by varnishing the radiator frames, giving the room a good cleaning, setting up beer kegs, winding up the phonograph, putting up paper ornaments, and placing the piano in the center of the room. After one of these, I found the beer keg by the front door and I tasted some of its contents, which were dripping from the spout. It was hardly enough to taste, but the smell of it was unmistakable.

The children from Műssen and Rohlsdorf would get together on multiple occasions. Our Műssen-Rohlsdorf track-and-field event was held during the late spring or early summer of 1948. We spent several weeks preparing for this competition. The events included the high jump, the broad jump, sack races, and many other events. My brother was one of the star athletes from the Műssen group, and we were soundly trounced by them. The event was great fun for all of us in spite of our defeat.

Birthday celebrations at the home were always joyful and exciting. For birthday gifts, children would receive crayons, pocket knives, 3-D sets, candy, and various other items.

Mrs. Zvēriņš discovered that Tolja and I did not know our birth dates. Once, when Tolja visited Rohlsdorf, it was finally decided that we would select our birthdays out of a bowl that contained slips of paper with different days of the year marked on them. I picked a paper that had December 11 on it and my brother's paper said September 3. Those dates have stuck to this day!

When December 11 came around she had a wonderful birthday party for me, and she surprised me with a collection of fine gifts. This included candy, chocolates, a wood erector set, sheets of decals that we used to decorate plates, a tiny mirror, a comb, a pencil, a small folding jackknife, and many other small items. We all craved pocket knives for carving wood, making whistles, bows and arrows, etc. I was thrilled and felt very special that day. The children sang the traditional "Happy Birthday" song to me, and I couldn't have been happier. I still remember that event quite vividly, and I will be forever grateful for Mrs. Zvēriņš' kindness and thoughtfulness toward me.

Life at Home in Rohlsdorf

Some nights I had difficulty controlling my bladder and bowel movements, and I would wake up in a soiled bed. They never scolded me for this, however. I believe many other children had the same problem.

To the south of our bedroom was a small bathroom that contained a bathtub, a sink, and a toilet. The water was usually quite rusty in color and many times we were without light and hot water. Marta, at first, washed and scrubbed us off from head to toe. But as she realized that we were becoming a bit self-conscious, she let us bathe on our own.

We learned to polish our shoes with a kit that was stored just inside the washroom. As part of our going-to-bed ritual, I would tell bedtime stories to the other boys. I would include the boys as heroes in these stories, which often had themes of war, fights, and foxholes. The boys seemed to enjoy these stories, so I kept telling them for many nights. Even today, when our grandchildren visit us, I tell them bedtime stories. This is a wonderful way to relate to children.

The dining room occupied a good part of the first floor. Our meals included liver, beef, pork, fish, rabbit, chicken, various kinds of vege- tables, soups, sausages, potatoes, puddings, cocoa, bread, butter, and jam. We were also given supplements to support our health, and these included chocolate-covered vitamin pills and cod-liver pills. Our meals tasted good and they were quite ample for us. We considered mushroom gravy to be a prized commodity in those days. Near the end of our stay here, we were also served puck-shaped cereal bars as a nutritional sup- plement. Those bars likely came from the United Nations. We were well fed, indeed!

There was a rabbit pen inside a cement closure not far from our building. Sometimes some of the men, including Antons, could be seen skinning the rabbits, withdrawing their entrails, and preparing them for the frying pan. This grieved me somewhat, because I had helped to feed these creatures and care for them. However, I did enjoy their meat in spite of this.

In the basement we found glass parts from a large chandelier. We got hold of some large glass balls that had been attached to the chandelier and used these in the sun to burn up flies. This "scientific experiment" soon came to an end, however, when the glass balls were taken from us. We also found some prisms, which we greatly enjoyed, and I still relish seeing the rainbowlike colors that prisms project from the sunshine.

Life in our Rohlsdorf home was usually peaceful and serene, and our counselors took good care of us there. I think it was great that they tried to keep us entertained, healthy, and well-educated. All in all, it was a wonderful place for us.

More Memories

While we were at Rohlsdorf, we had the opportunity to visit a one-ringed circus in a tent not far away. I remember seeing the colorful circus wagons that encircled the tent. The circus itself had several different acts, including trained horses that ran around the inner circle and did some stunts, acrobats who did gymnastics from a high ladder, a man balancing a boy, dog stunts, and various other events. We had the opportunity to ride on the back of a pony, but I was afraid to do so, for I had seen some of the children fall off.

Another time we went to a fair where we saw an organ grinder and the booths of various vendors who sold things like buttons, safety pins, thimbles, and the like. We went on some of the rides, including the swiveling chair and the May-pole type carousel that had seats that lifted as the speed increased.

Sometimes we would do knitting in our free time at the home. Believe it or not, I thought this was fun, though I don't remember making anything that was particularly useful or significant. We learned how to thread a button between two strings and then we could spin it back and forth. We also played a game with string in which we could make various designs as we transferred it back and forth between the fingers of a partner to our own and back.

We did some destructive things, as well, such as when we would take out the screw contacts in the plug-ins. We would sometimes kick these loose in order to avoid being electrocuted. Then we would insert pins into the outlets and poke each other with them. When the adults found out what we were doing, these "games" were immediately prohibited.

Regarding religion, I picked up some rather strange ideas at Rohlsdorf. Some of these I've already mentioned, such as God riding in a chariot during thunderstorms. I wondered if some of these things were true. Did the devil live in the fiery depths of the Earth? Somehow I thought that each of us is a small portion of God. This led to the conclusion that the more people there are, there is less and less of God!

I also believed that one day I would find a magic ring or object that would be able to produce anything I wanted. (I'm sure this thought came from many stories that I read and that were read to us.) I also believed that if I were condemned to eternal punishment, Jesus would come to hell every Easter to rescue me and restore me to Heaven. Some of these deceptions were actually taught to us and it took considerable effort to extricate myself from them.

We became amateur botanists in Rohlsdorf. We learned to like certain plants, the shoots of grasses, and the sweet nectar of clover plants. We ate the light-green leaves of a clover-like plant that tasted a bit like lettuce. We took pods from a certain kind of bush and used these inch-long, pea-like structures to blow through, making very loud noises.

We learned how to make noises in other ways, as well. For example, we would place pieces of grass between our cupped hands and blow, and we would take leather belts, double them up, and snap them. We learned that sticks with ropes would make a loud cracking sound when they were whipped swiftly, and we turned whistling through the holes of a hollow metal button into "music."

During a visit to Müssen, my brother showed me a piece of glowing wood. Tolja was an extrovert and I was an introvert, and this may have been part of the reason why we clashed so much when we were together.

On November 18, 1948, we celebrated the thirtieth anniversary of Latvia's independence. The commemoration of independence day at Müssen was a big event. We spent quite a bit of time in preparation for the celebration by rehearsing songs while one of the Müssen counselors played the violin. Multicolored balloons were hung from the ceiling of the ballroom and chandelier. We were dressed in our finest clothing. One of the Müssen instructors took powder-flash gun photographs with a device that aroused our curiosity because we had never seen anything like it before.

At this time Latvia was under the control of the Soviet Union, but Latvians continued to hope and pray for their nation's recovery of independence, which took place finally in 1990.

Some distinguished-looking Latvian men ignited four or five cylindrical containers. The result was the most beautiful display of fireworks I had ever seen. They put forth red, blue, and green flares and sparks. We sang patriotic songs and danced in celebration of this major event.

Back home at Rohlsdorf, a Latvian visitor took several of us aside and asked, "Has anyone ever told you how the Latvian flag came about?" We all said no. He then expressed his concern that we should learn the story correctly. He then went on to explain that during a historic battle in Latvia, a commander had been seriously wounded. He was placed in a sheet, which became soaked red with his blood, except for a white stripe down the middle where he laid. Upon his death, his men took up the sheet and used it as their banner, and their zeal won them the victory. I have never heard any other explanation of the design of the Latvian flag.

I loved learning all I could about my homeland—a country on the Baltic Sea between Lithuania and Estonia. Its landscape is marked by wide beaches and dense, sprawling forests. The capital of Latvia is Rīga, the home to wooden and art-nouveau architecture, a vast central market, some very old churches, and a medieval old town. It is a wonderful place to visit.

Personal Reflections

I was about to be "uprooted" once more. My next home would be Klingenberg, a town in Bavaria. My brother stayed behind at Müssen. As I understand it, my going to Klingenberg was due to the fact that I had graduated from the third grade at Rohlsdorf. Apparently the teachers at Rohlsdorf thought I would receive more thorough instruction at Klingenberg, and as you will see in the next chapter, they were right. Whereas I had begun to plant the roots of my life into the soil of relationships and existence in Rohlsdorf, I would soon be uprooted and transplanted. It was not possible for me to feel settled again until I was finally adopted by the Rev. and Mrs. Victor C. Boe in June 1950.

Even though my childhood had many difficulties, I feel quite fortunate. I realize I could have been brought up in a dysfunctional home with drug-saturated, alcoholic parents, as many children have. These bad influences can grow, causing children to have personality defects and addictions of their own.

Can such early behavioral traits be intercepted and converted into positive, productive influences? The apostle Paul would have said YES. He regarded himself as the worst of the worst, for he had been the murderer of Christians among many other things.

We must never give up on anyone. We must love them by praying for them, being there for them, listening to them, and leading them to the Light.

Paul wrote, "Therefore, if anyone is in Christ, he is a new creation; old things have been passed away; behold, all things have become new".

(2 CORINTHIANS 5:17, NKJV)

CHAPTER 7

KLINGENBERG

A Thatched-Roof House

In Klingenberg our home was a three-story, thatch-roofed house with an attic that was exposed to the weather and was occupied by an owl. There was a two-room medical center on the first floor and it was staffed by a regular nurse. It was here where we were weighed, our blood pressure was measured, our blood samples were taken, and we received various shots. Our cuts and bruises were treated here, as well. I remember that the nurse and I got along nicely.

Between ten and fifteen children lived here. We slept on the second floor, in a couple of rooms on single beds. Apparently one of my roommates was a German, and I remember that he had a German storybook that contained stories of weird, man-choking serpents that had large, snakelike tentacles. These creatures would spend their time surprising human beings and frightening them, and I was led to believe that they actually existed. As you can imagine, this scared me quite a lot.

The wind would make howling noises through the cracks in the window of our room. This haunting sound, particularly during thunderstorms, would make me shudder with fear. Some of the old fears I had experienced during World War II had been put to rest, but new ones were waiting for me.

Klingenberg, Germany, 1948

Folk Tales, Myths, and Stories

Mr. Jēcabsons seemed to be the chief counselor at the Klingenberg home. He lived with his wife and young son in an apartment across from our room. Mr. Jēcabsons was a heavyset, light-haired, fatherly but firm man with whom we spent many evenings in the well-equipped living room on the first floor. It was the closest I had ever been to being a part of a family.

It was a very homey setting for us. There was a grand piano in the corner and I remember the beautiful stained-glass windows in the living room. It was in this room where our counselor read many Latvian tales to us, and these always captured my interest and attention. These included stories of witches and haunted houses, young men pursuing beautiful damsels, people who outwitted the devil, finding magical rings that enabled the finders to have whatever they wanted, and many other fascinating themes.

One explanatory myth involved a man who needed a pinch of salt for his dinner, and he happened to come upon a wizard who handed him a small box with a wind-up level that turned around and around. By using magical words this would produce salt. But the man forgot the magical words, and he threw it into the ocean where it continues to churn out salt without stopping!

Another story concerned a young man who descended into a deep hole by means of a basket in order to rescue his damsel from the clutches of the devil. Though he found her busily knitting when he got there, he managed to convince her to go with him, and they thereby avoided the approaching devil and his agent by changing into sheep first and then into flies.

I remember also the story of a one-eyed giant who had trapped a number of men in a cave. His plan was to keep them there until he could devour them. The hero of this story succeeded in knocking out this giant's one eye, and this enabled the men to escape from the cave by hiding under the giant's sheep as they were let out to pasture. There was another story of a man who could play his fiddle so well that crowds would gather around him, and he would make them cry or laugh. We also read many stories about animal characters—such as wolves, foxes, crows, and others—that were against animals that seemed more innocent—such as rabbits, chickens, dogs, cats, etc.

Mr. Jēcabsons told us that in Latvia he had gone around telling such stories just to get a cup of coffee from people at various homes and other places. He always enjoyed partaking of fellowship with other people. He told these stories with such conviction that it made it impossible for us to figure out which tales were true and which were totally fictional.

One Christmas he told us that Santa and his reindeer and sleigh could be seen riding by at any time, and he would deposit the toys in a special box outside the house. He dared us to go out into the cold night and the snow to find out. Instead, we took his word for it, although I must admit I had my doubts, but it was much nicer to stay indoors in the warmth.

Mr. Jēcabsons could play the piano quite well and frequently led us in singing. All in all, it was a very pleasant atmosphere for us. Our father figure had become our friend, and yet he demanded our respect. His superior size and strength may have had something to do with this. His wife was very kind to us, as well, but she had no responsibility over us.

Other People in Our Home

There were a couple of apartments upstairs. Mr. and Mrs. Mežaks lived in one section. Mrs. Mežaks had been a fellow student with Rose in Latvia and had also served in the Majori home. She told me that the chief reason why we were turned over to the Baldone home was due to the acute poverty of our mother, who apparently did not have enough money to even get bread and butter for herself. This reminded me of the story of Hansel and Gretel.

She taught us a measure of stewardship by paying us a little bit each time we carried coal for her in a coal bucket from the basement. I managed to save enough money to buy a tennis ball, a plastic pencil sharpener, a tablet of paper, and pencils at a small shop near our home. This was a new experience for me—buying things for myself with my own money, and I must admit that I enjoyed the feeling of self-assurance and independence this gave to me.

The other apartment was occupied by my main instructor. This man, whose name I am not sure of, was responsible for teaching me English, Latvian history, arithmetic, and other subjects. I remember how we made a clay-relief map of Latvia, which showed the mountains, rivers, and lakes of our country. I greatly enjoyed such projects, especially those that involved working with my hands.

Our situation was complicated by the fact that there was a community of Lithuanians who lived to the south of our home. At first we would hike over to their home for meals. The main menu there consisted of various kinds of soups, along with cottage-cheese-and-jelly sandwiches.

Due to the language barrier we never really got to know the Lithuanian children very well. At times our relationship with them even grew to be hostile and competitive. During the winter, however, we did get together near their home for skiing, sliding, and sledding on the nearby lake.

After we were given a weekly allowance of German currency with which to "purchase" used and new toys in a distribution center, the children in our home all thought that the Lithuanians got bigger and better toys than we did. That might very well have been the case, in that they usually had first choice when it came to toy selection. Some of my "purchases" included a small flashlight with a magnifying type of lens, which actually worked until the batteries wore out, and a small toy truck.

There were a number of older youths who must not have been part of the original 130 who left Majori. These boys were a grade or two above me.

Klingenberg, Germany, 1948, after attending church service

Same photo of lesser quality, Volodja is circled on the right,
Tolja circled on the left, note pastor to Volodja's right

Francis and Scouting

One man who had a great influence on my life in Klingenberg was called
Francis. We assumed that he was a Frenchman. It was he who organized
a rather primitive scout troop and led us on numerous hikes in the vicinity to the east of our home. In that direction was a playing field that was
a long, flat, football-sized depression with goal posts at both ends. We
played some organized games here, including hide-and-seek. I remember
that one of the boys was expelled from our group because he persisted in
being mean and kicking others.

During one of our hikes we went to an area that was filled with young
evergreens and guarded by a dog and its owner. Apparently someone had
gotten into this nursery-like, fenced-in area and chopped down some of
these beautiful young trees. Whoever did this mischief simply left the
chopped-down trees lying there. We asked for permission to take these
with us, for we would often burn branches and bake potatoes under the
hot coals, a delicious treat for us. Permission to do so was granted.

We became accustomed to running down the steep drop to the south of our home and up the other slope. It was good exercise for us. Both slopes became quite bare and beaten down. During the winter months we would slide down the opposite slope. An open stream of sewage emptied from the house and ran down to the creek at the base of the slope. I can still recall its unpleasant smell, which we could detect from a great distance away. Occasionally we would step into this smelly stuff, though generally we avoided it. Once, a delivery truck slid down the slope behind our house, and another truck with an electrical winch on its front pulled it out with a cable.

There was a wide, graveled approach to the west of our building. As we would walk along this road, we would first pass an old hand pump on the right. It worked when it was not frozen. At the corner on the right, there was a dilapidated shed, which was occupied by a cat. I wondered how the cat survived in such cold weather, but it somehow managed to do so.

The graveled driveway led to the main road. Our power line with completely bare lines followed the same path. Whenever a tree branch fell on these lines, our lights in the home would flicker and go out. Eventually these lines were replaced with shiny, red copper wires, which served us much better.

All along the way there were dogs. Many of them were German shepherds, and they would bark almost in unison when we approached. One of these dogs was chained, and it snarled, growled, and leaped at us so violently that I feared to think what might happen if it ever tore loose. Fortunately, it never did.

Some of the older youths rented bicycles and rode along the road at their leisure. This was a privilege that the rest of us greatly envied. While walking through the wooded area on the right, we saw an elderly man hauling some old stumps in a wheelbarrow. Despite his age and his fragile appearance, he had dug up these stumps with a shovel by himself. I am sure he was planning to use them for fuel.

Logging operations kept up a steady pace in this region. I noticed that the loggers had a trailer of sorts for their bunkhouse and chow center. Large trees were hauled out even from the swampy area near the lake.

On one of our excursions through this area we came upon some relics of war—a German helmet and empty gun shells. This was a fearful reminder of what we all had been through not that long ago. During the warmer months the lake would be rather tumultuous, with furious waves pounding against the cement embankment near the shore. In the winter, though, ice covered the lake and we were able to explore the shorelines and docks at ease.

There were two-story brick buildings across a little foot bridge, and it was my understanding that these houses were for veterans of the war. As we would continue walking, I would always hope to see animals that were larger than squirrels and rabbits, but this never happened. Actually, I'm glad we never saw wolves or bears!

We would cross a large steel bridge. On the other side was a small town that had several brick shops and buildings. We noticed that a new factory was being built there, and I heard that it was to become a chalk factory. There was a swift-flowing stream that ran through the town. Someone told us that a person was killed in this stream when a downed power line fell into it. A person who tried to bring about his rescue was killed also. This may have simply been our elders' way of telling us to be careful, but the story left quite an impression on me.

We saw several shops as we walked through the town. One was a beauty salon. Then we came to a train station. As we continued past these buildings, we came to an area that was closed off by a large metal fence. On the hill above us, I could see a large brick building, which we believed to be a prison. We were permitted to walk up to and around that building several times, but I never saw very many people there.

Continuing past this place we would pass a lone, tall power pole with a transformer. I remember wondering what would happen if this large tower fell on top of us! Farther down the highway to the left, we saw a large, closed-in, water-filled area that we thought might have been used to raise fish.

Straight ahead of us was the seashore with a beach that had various kinds of shells and water plants. It was a rather smelly place due to the dead seaweed on the shore, which had bean-sized berries that smelled badly, as well. It was not a good place for swimming, but it was nonetheless refreshing to be near the sea.

After we left this area and continued straight ahead we came to a cemetery. During one war-memorial day we were instructed to be solemn and respectful while we were there. We saw some women bringing flowers to the graves. It was a well-maintained cemetery, but there were few tombstones there. On the other side of the cemetery we saw some concrete structures with locked doors. Someone told us that these may have been used for mass burials.

If, instead of crossing the highway, we would take a road to the left, we would come to a hill with many small evergreens. Our leader would point in the direction of the city, which could be seen clearly from this vantage point, weather permitting. On the particular day when we were there, however, it was drizzling rain so it was hard to see the city.

A main power line ran through this area. It was supported by metal-frame towers, and we were told not to get near these. Our leaders warned us that a bird straddling any two wires would be burned to a crisp! The workers there also warned us to stay away from these towers.

Back at Home

When we returned home we would come to a main complex of buildings. First, we would pass a small wooden building where my classes were conducted in a rather small and crowded room. There were other rooms in this same building, which served as offices and apartments. One of the women there introduced us to some of her homemade tea, which consisted of a number of leaves and ingredients from the surrounding area. Surprisingly, it tasted good to me even though I had no idea where the leaves had come from.

There was an outside latrine that was open to the air. It contained a long metal trough that we were supposed to use. There was apparently no flushing mechanism, though. For bowel movements, the kids would most often use the woods. A stench that was almost unbearable filled the air within and around the latrine. I remember wondering if a pigpen might have been more pleasant!

This reminds me of a time at Rohlsdorf, when a pig got loose and was cornered by some boys. The poor animal was almost completely exhausted by the chase, and a local farmer came to rescue the animal and to warn us against doing the same thing again.

I believe we had a small pigpen at the back of our dining-room building in Klingenberg. Once, when one of these pigs was being caught in order to be slaughtered for meat, it got away and it took several of us to capture it so we could have our stew!

Beyond the latrine, there was a wooden hall where we went for movies and lectures. One of our chief lecturers was Mrs. Mežaks. She would read from newspaper articles in order to point out a certain moral and would ask us questions about it to see how well we were listening. Sometimes these talks were more like indoctrination speeches than lectures.

I remember our last lecture in this hall, for it was especially intense and was designed to instill in us a nationalistic zeal. On a table near us was a picture of a freight car with very small openings at the top. The openings had iron bars over them. Through these we could see the faces and arms of people who were desperately reaching out for air and freedom, but we were told they were bound for Siberia, a long and arduous journey that would lead to the deaths of many of them.

We were told that thousands of Latvians had been transported to Siberia in such freight cars. Those who survived the trip were put in slave camps in that cold and barren part of Russia!

The dining hall served a variety of foods, including potato and vegetable soup—one of my favorites. They also served us cottage cheese, homemade white and dark breads, sauerkraut (so much so that I still can't stomach it!), vegetables, pudding, and the like.

Once when I was in the kitchen, I noticed that the cook used large quantities of vinegar, which helped to preserve the food. A local farmer would come by the kitchen from time to time to pick up potato peels and other leftovers to use as hog "slop." Sometimes he would untie his horse from the wagon and hitch it up near the building, and the children would try to pet it. However, the horse was not too friendly and, once, he kicked one of the children; this put an end to us going near him ever again.

Thinking about America

I knew I was in the final days of my time in Klingenberg, and that, in all likelihood, I would be going to the United States of America in the near future. This thought both thrilled and scared me, but I was looking forward to it. It seemed so far away, so huge, and so unknown to us. Would I do well there?

Zigrīda Brūders' apartment was upstairs. I hadn't noticed her much, but not long before I left the home, she invited me to her room to show me some photographs. I asked her if she would give me one of the pictures of herself. I promised to write her once I got to America. She complied with my request, but I remember her saying that I would likely forget her once I got settled in my future home.

Zigrīda Brūders, 1947 or 1948

Eventually I got her address from Rose and I did write to her from America. She wrote back, saying that she was thrilled to receive my letter. She tried to find a small pin with the Latvian flag on it to give to me, but she was unsuccessful. However, she did send me several small gifts. As our correspondence went on, I learned that she had served as a cook or a waitress in a restaurant in Eutin, Germany, not far from Malente.

To the north of our building was a country road, which we took once in order to attend a Christmas party. Our destination was a large community hall. We were directed to chairs that had been placed in a circle. After we got adjusted and began singing Christmas carols, in came Santa Claus! He was wearing a bright-red suit and hat, and had a long white beard. He was carrying a large sack on his back. This was the first time I had ever seen "the old man of Christmas," *Ziemsvetku Vecis*, although I had heard much about him. Each of us was given a small bag of surprises, and in mine there was a small mirror and a comb. (Adults would sometimes tease us by asking, "Would you like to see a monkey?" We would answer, "What does one look like?" They would tell us to look in the mirror and then they would say, "There is the monkey!")

It was such a delightful evening for all of us. We were filled with joy as we sang Christmas songs and received gifts from Santa Claus.

A couple of times professional puppet troupes would entertain us. Sometimes the puppet figures looked real enough that they did not seem artificial at all. At other times it was apparent that the puppeteers were using their hands and fingers to manipulate the puppets. During some changes of scene in the shows an accordion would be played.

Lübeck continued to be our main health center, and we would go there for any required medical treatment. We were told that one of our children had swallowed a key and was in great danger. They asked us to pray for him so that an operation would not be necessary. We heard later that he had successfully passed the key in a bowel movement. I wondered then if God had heard our prayers and performed a miracle on his behalf.

During one of our final meals at the home, the topic of bread came up. One of the women reminded us that we should eat plenty of dark bread, because when we got to America, they would serve us nutrient-deficient white bread. She said we would get sick of white bread and plead for dark bread again. This was not the case with me, however, for I have come to like both white and dark bread.

After Christmas, various preparations were being made for our trip to America. We learned that not all would go to the United States, however. Some would remain in Germany due to physical ailments and other concerns.

One of the first things we had to do was to get our pictures taken. Next, we had to have our fingerprints taken. Radiographs of our bodies were obtained on several different occasions. Most of these examinations were done at Wentorf, where there was a large complex of medical buildings. I worried about this for a bit because of my earlier bout with tuberculosis, but apparently the doctors thought I had improved sufficiently to go ahead with the trip to the United States.

As farewell presents, we were given autographed books and photographs. One of the ladies, thinking that I was more advanced in reading than I really was, purchased a very difficult storybook for me. I found it too hard to read.

Shortly before our departure, we returned to Rohlsdorf. We were surprised to see the building in such a mess due to the fact that the adults had been gathering and packing their possessions for the big move. I got to see my brother here, and he was very excited about the prospect of moving. Since I had left the Rohlsdorf home they had taken in some juvenile delinquents who had proved to be quite unmanageable and incorrigible. When I learned this I was glad that I had not stayed there!

As we traveled, I noticed windmills. Some had been abandoned, but others were still in use. I took mental pictures of these, because I thought I might never see them again.

A night or two before our final departure, we were given long, white duffle bags. We were told to put our most cherished possessions and clothing in these. We had also been given some new items of clothing. All of our earthly possessions that we valued would be going with us.

We would soon be on our way. We dreamed about America, and what we might experience when we got there. Would we be adopted? Would we go to school? Would we make new friends? Would life get better for us? It was all very exciting and a bit overwhelming.

Personal Reflections

We had moved so many times in the past, but the upcoming move seemed particularly significant. We knew that America was a big country that was filled with many wonderful things to see and do. I was particularly interested in seeing New York City and the Statue of Liberty.

I made up my mind that I would approach this move with a positive attitude. I was very grateful for this new opportunity, and I wanted to make the best of it. I told myself to be strong and courageous, and to rise above my fear. I was expecting good things to happen, and I was so happy to get away from the war-torn land that had been all I knew. The Holocaust was now behind me, and a bright future was just around the corner. To me, America would be the greatest gift I'd ever received.

CHAPTER 8

A NEW WORLD ACROSS
THE ATLANTIC

For God has not given us a spirit of fear,
but of power and of love and of a sound mind.
(2 TIMOTHY 1:7, NKJV)

To think of flying across the Atlantic Ocean and going to America was truly exhilarating for me. I had no idea what would happen to us once we got there, but I dreamed of many wonderful things. America had been portrayed to me as being a vast country that was filled with opportunity.

Our first stop would be Hamburg, in northern Germany. It all seemed to happen so suddenly. We were loaded into trucks and were on our way to Hamburg. As we headed north, I noticed a beautiful automobile behind us. It had a very fancy chrome grill that dazzled in the sunlight. I admired it and wondered what it would be like to ride in such a vehicle.

As we neared Hamburg, we passed blocks and blocks of gutted brick buildings and piles of rubble along the streets. It seemed as if hardly any buildings were intact. It had been a relatively long time since the end of

World War II, but there was still a great deal of evidence of warfare that had taken place all over the area.

Our final stop on this truck ride was the airport. We entered the terminal, and they processed our bags and put identification tags on us. The trip of a lifetime was about to begin! I was both excited and a bit fearful, but I was certain that great things were in store for me.

Above the Clouds

As we were in the waiting room, we received packages from the Red Cross. We watched as a large plane was being prepared for takeoff. I wondered if this would be our airplane. We boarded that very plane and soon the doors were closed behind us. Many of the adults remained behind and I could see them standing by the building. I knew I would miss them, but the separation was not particularly traumatic, at least not to me.

Hamburg, Germany Airport, on way to America, March 1949

Hamburg Airport

Slowly the engines started up. As they warmed up, the pitch of the engines' noise grew to a crescendo and we knew it would soon be time to take off. The plane began to move down the runway. The counselors who did not go with us were waving at us with their handkerchiefs, and we waved back.

Shortly thereafter the airplane was off the ground. I was taking in every moment with a feeling of great excitement. The plane climbed higher and higher, and eventually we were above the clouds. They were white and puffy, and it seemed as if they were the peaks of mountains. Through my imagination I could make out faces, animals, and other things as I stared at them.

Before long, however, darkness came and I could no longer see anything, except for the sparks and flames of the motors. We wondered, *What if an engine caught fire, burned up, and fell off?* Some of the children fell asleep. Others were airsick and they began to vomit. I experienced a rumble in my stomach, but I was able to keep from throwing up. We were not given anything to eat, but we did receive cups of water and juice.

I opened the box that the Red Cross had given to me, and found that it contained soap, a tube of toothpaste, a toothbrush, pencils, a comb, a small mirror, and a couple of small toys.

I was surprised when the plane began to descend and we landed in Iceland. As we disembarked, we noticed that the weather was damp and cold.

In the terminal building, we gathered briefly in the main corridor. It was here where I saw Francis for the last time. We were then ushered into a small room and given some instructions by a uniformed British official. He explained that we were in Iceland, and pointed to a large wall map that showed this island nation. We learned that Iceland had an ample supply of geothermal heat, which was used for heating homes, etc.

We then went into a dining area and enjoyed egg-salad sandwiches before we got back on the plane to resume our journey. I went back to the same seat I had before and looked out of the window. The snow on the ground glowed from the lights of the building and the plane. The whole airport seemed spectacular, with many rows of lights going in different directions. We noticed a TWA plane nearby with its engines roaring. I marveled at its distinct design. The plane stood high on its wheels, with its two propellers blaring loudly. Its split tail assembly was very distinct from other airlines. The propellers did emit sparks that were conspicuously visible at night and left scorch marks on the wings.

After we took off we were soon above the ocean once again. I continued to notice that the airplane's engines emitted quite a few sparks and I wondered whether this was normal. I hoped they would not catch fire. Soon thereafter, though, I relaxed and fell asleep.

When I awoke, the dawn of the new day had come. As I peered below, I could not see many clouds. It seemed as if the entire area within my vision was a sheet of ice, and I could even see cracks in its surface. I wondered what would happen if the plane crashed and we would have to be rescued in such a cold and barren environment.

It was not long, however, before we saw the faint, green outline of a land mass in the distance. It took a while to get there, though. As the plane began its initial descent, we knew we were above New York City. At first we passed over some white oil-storage tanks. Then we went over tall skyscrapers, including the Empire State Building, which I had seen in photos when I was in Germany.

We approached and landed on the tarmac of the city airport, which was known as the international airport and is now the site of the Kennedy International Airport. We disembarked and were greeted by a host of photographers and newsmen. We were told to pose for photographs. It was all very strange to me.

We entered the terminal and were interviewed by a number of reporters with microphones and tape recorders, and there was a mass of wires everywhere. I did not know enough English at that time to be able to understand what they were asking or to respond to their questions. In some ways this made me feel left out of the excitement of the moment.

Soon some ladies came and escorted us out of the building and into waiting automobiles that were probably taxi cabs. This was the first time I had ever been in an automobile! The ladies assured us that we would be well taken care of and that we would be able to take nice, hot baths when we reached our destination.

New York City

We had arrived in New York during the early spring. While we were there only one light snowfall took place.

Our new, temporary residence was a tall brick building in a residential section of the city. There were a few shops in the building and surrounding vicinity. People gave us pennies, which we used to buy popsicles, candy, and chewing gum. The next day we saw an ice-cream vendor come along on his bicycle and wagon, ringing his bell. When we understood what he was doing, we had to purchase ice-cream bars from him. We soon came to recognize the sound of the bell that announced the arrival of the ice-cream wagon, and whenever we heard it, we would go immediately to buy our favorite ice-cream bars or cones.

We were fed huge, delicious meals in our new residence. We had all the big, bright oranges we desired to eat. We drank milk from clean, square-top cartons. Our food consisted of potatoes, meat, gravy, and vegetables, and we could have as much as we wanted. We were given navy-blue coats, which were quite warm and comfortable. We had never been "spoiled" like this before!

In my bedroom upstairs I unpacked my belongings. I don't think we had ever slept so soundly and comfortably before. We began to feel like citizens who belonged to this new and wonderful community, and we began to take all these luxuries and conveniences in stride. I had a sense that America was a very prosperous country and that I would like it.

Happiness does not come from things, however, and our excitement over all that had been given to us soon began to die down. We were now in the United States, and it certainly appeared to be as wonderful as we had thought it would be. When I first heard of America (or "Usa," as I had thought it was pronounced when I saw it on a stamp in Rohlsdorf), I thought it was a country of prosperity.

As time went on, the second group of children from Germany finally arrived. When I asked Maija why they had arrived so long after us, she explained that they had to come across the ocean by ship. That seemed logical to me, and she told me about the pleasures they had while aboard the ship. I wondered if I would have enjoyed coming over by ship more than by plane. (It was several years later when I learned that the others had come by airplane, as well, and I wondered why Maija had told me that story.)

We enjoyed visiting the sites in this great city. We had been given identification bracelets, but I had lost mine soon after getting it. I was particularly impressed by New York at nighttime. There were so many multicolored lights everywhere. At one spot I saw a large waterfall flowing over a high wall. We even became accustomed to riding the subway as we went from place to place, and I was greatly fascinated by this means of transportation and overhead railways.

One of the first American songs we learned was "Home, Home on the Range." This seemed to be an idyllic portrayal of life in America. From the movies and pictures we had seen, it had seemed to us that America was a land of cowboys and Indians. Certainly the life I did come to experience in America was truly idyllic (minus the cowboys and Indians), a far cry from the devastation of war in Europe from which we had emerged. I recall so vividly the rubble that lined the streets of Hamburg as we prepared to leave. How thankful I was that the Holocaust was behind us.

I came to enjoy family life and schooling opportunities that had not been available to me in Europe. I praise God that none of our children or grandchildren have had to suffer the same horrors of war, though our youngest son and his wife (Steven and Dana) served with the U.S. Navy in Iraq during war, and that must have been very scary indeed.

Let us pray that all of us and our families will be spared the horrors and conflicts of war and devastation, but we must keep in mind that the greatest conflict of all is within us. (Read Ephesians 2:14–16.) Jesus broke down the inner wall that divided and separated us, making us one in Him.

We walked across the Brooklyn Bridge and were told about its construction. We went through a park with green lawns and many trees. While we were at a playground, I took notice of traffic lights that controlled the constant flow of trucks and automobiles. We visited the zoo and were thrilled to see the various animals that were there.

We went to an island from which we were able to view the skyline of Manhattan. While there, I had my first taste of peanuts and tried to eat the whole bag, but this made me violently ill, so I have stayed away from peanuts since then. I found it interesting to walk on sidewalks that had circular pieces of purple glass in them. I learned that these brought light to rooms below.

It was quite an experience to ride the subway and to get on or off the trains via underground stations. I noticed signs with the word "Hamburg" on them, and I wondered what that was all about. When I was told about hamburgers, I was still puzzled over how these sandwiches got their name. I couldn't figure out what the city of Hamburg had to do with them. (Since then I've learned that the word "hamburger" does come from the seaport town of Hamburg, Germany. It is thought that nineteenth-century sailors brought back the idea of raw shredded beef, which is now known as beef tartare, after trading with the Baltic provinces of Russia.)

Our counselors tried to teach us about the American way of life, and in doing so, they taught us some American history. I remember them asking us what a cowboy is, and I ventured an answer: "It is a boy who rides on a cow." Of course, I was corrected about this.

We saw many movies, some of which were cartoons and slapstick comedies, which we found to be very funny indeed. Some of these had surprisingly violent themes, such as a man lighting a match and holding it above a gas tank to see if there was any gas in it, followed by a huge explosion. In one of the offices was a television set, which we would be able to view from time to time.

Some of the children were adopted right from this residence. One of these was David Stiprais, a Jewish boy. After his soon-to-be adoptive father had visited him, David said that he had been promised a brand-new bicycle and some spending money. This seemed amazing to the rest of us.

I began to wonder on what basis adoptions were considered. Maybe David's adoptive parents were Jews. Were children adopted because of their looks? Their intelligence? Their background? Their religion? I was so eager to be adopted myself, but I had no alternative but to keep on waiting.

Along some of our walks I would pick up a cigarette butt that was still lighted and take a puff on it. Later I was led to believe that my "smoking" may have stunted my growth.

We never got to go inside the Empire State Building, but I did try counting the number of floors in the building from the outside. I gave up after I reached fifty floors.

We learned that we would have to leave New York soon. We were given cardboard suitcases and new suits. By this time, I had very little left of what I had brought to America from Europe except for some stamps, books, and photos.

We got into Checker cabs and headed to the airport. We boarded a two-engine United Airlines plane. It was much more comfortable than the last airplane we were on. While we were in the air we were served a sumptuous meal that consisted of hot meat, potatoes, and vegetables, along with a fruit dessert.

As I looked out from the window, it seemed as if the terrain below was quite rugged. I was looking at the Appalachian Mountains, which seemed like mole hills from that height. At one point we saw a fire in a town below, and the smoke from this fire seemed to reach the airplane itself.

We landed at the Milwaukee, Wisconsin, airport. My bladder was full at this point, and I wet my pants as they were taking photographs of us! I remember trying to hide the wet spot on my trousers from the photographers. Some of the children disembarked in Milwaukee.

DP orphan children arriving for resettlement in USA under auspices of National Lutheran Council. Right, the Bernadotte Medal, presented to LWF by the Red Cross

Milwaukee, Wisconsin Airport, note Volodja waving by stairs

The remaining children were then transferred to Minneapolis, Minnesota. We were placed under the Lutheran World Action program that dealt with refugees and displaced persons, which included temporary foster homes and facilitation of adoption. There were six of us children altogether, including me and my brother, Vilnis Vibants, Tiit, Bruno, and Karlis. We were taken to the Hoikka residence in St. Paul Park, St. Paul, Minnesota. From this point on we would be under the supervision of

Miss Evelyn Schaefer and Mr. James Raun from the Lutheran Welfare Office in St. Paul.

St Paul Park, MN, summer 1949, at Anna and Jack Hoikka's

After we arrived in St. Paul, Minnesota, the Jewish Welfare Agency, having learned about our arrival, inquired to the Lutheran Social Services about our ID and jurisdictional status. A date was arranged for a meeting, but it was soon canceled. There was no documentation and no proof or our ID. A kindly, elderly Jewish woman one day brought me a cardboard suitcase that was filled with clothing. I thanked her for her kindness.

Our identity was not questioned again until 2007, when family members wanted to learn of our family origins. This was when our likely Jewish ancestry was disclosed and confirmed for the first time. When we visited Washington, D.C., we learned that our names are listed in the Holocaust Museum there on the Survivors' List. It also disclosed my hospitalization for tuberculosis.

The Hoikka Residence

Our house was located about a half mile from the Mississippi River. It was the home of the Hoikka family. They were fond of rock gardens and they had several around their house. They had a huge pile of manure in the back, which they used to fertilize their gardens.

Mr. Jack Hoikka had a horse at one time, and there was a sleigh in the small barn not far from the pile of manure. This area was infested with mice and rabbits. Fortunately, the manure was far enough away from the house to keep the unpleasant aroma away.

Our bedroom was on the second floor. They wisely placed rubber sheets under the regular sheets in the event of nighttime "accidents," and this was probably a good idea considering our history. Our group of boys did not get along with each other particularly well, except when we were engaged in activities that kept us individually occupied.

One activity we enjoyed was catching small sunfish with our hands in the bay. We would fry the small fish and eat them. Mrs. Anna Hoikka recalled that we went "skinny dipping" occasionally in the muddy bay, and we would spend much time rowing in the boat.

Bob, an older boy with a glass eye living in the Hoikka foster home, often went spearing for carp in the swamps along the stream. He would catch large snapping turtles that a neighbor regarded as a true delicacy when they were used in soup. Both he and Howard, another older youth who had been at the home before we arrived, fished for bullheads at the point where the bay joined the stream. One evening Bob took me along in the rowboat. We went a good way from the house. Mrs. Hoikka had warned him about not going too far, but he kept testing the depth of the stream with his oar and assuring me that the stream was not too deep.

We explored a muddy area that had a lot of scraggy trees in it. Darkness came all too quickly that evening, and by the time we were headed back home it was completely dark and I was startled by the fire-flies that seemed to be everywhere. This reminded me of an experience I had had in Sierksdorf, and it frightened me. Mrs. Hoikka scolded us for staying out so late and going so far.

Bob had an air rifle; one day, while we were teasing him, he shot right at us! The BB's hit me in the back and on my belt. He did the same thing again when we were on the bay on another day.

Soon after we arrived at the home, I noticed that some of my prized possessions, particularly pencils, were missing. A teenaged girl admitted to taking these, because she thought they were hers. She promised to return them, but she never did.

To keep myself busy I would play with a large metal truck on the east side of the house. I would also pick gooseberries from a nearby bush. As I did so, I would crush them with my hands and make "jam" out of them for midday snacks. Another favorite spread for bread, though, was the delicious apple butter.

Mrs. Hoikka had a player piano in the main room, and she took great care to keep me and the others away from it. One day, though, I turned on the large console radio, and sometime later she found that the transformer was smoking from overheating! She proceeded to blame me for tampering with the radio.

There were a few elderly people who stayed in the home, as well. Most of the time, they just sat there, silent and inactive, seldom talking. That was how they spent their time, day after day.

On one occasion we caught a small injured rabbit, put it in a small cage, and tried to feed it. Despite our attempts to care for it, it soon died and we buried it in the field to the west of the house. We put up a tiny cross that was made of sticks to mark the grave.

The only child of the Hoikkas was Curtis, who was about college age. He operated a filling station about a mile away from the home. Eventually he purchased a fancy speed boat with a trailer and, after putting it in the water in the bay, took us for a thrilling ride along the Mississippi.

There were a number of garter snakes along the bay, and I feared even the sight of them. I remember once when Bob picked one up by the tail and swung it around to show that he was not afraid of snakes. Then he knocked off its head. Mrs. Hoikka tried to convince us that these snakes were harmless and were, in fact, quite useful in that they killed rodents and other pests. Even so, there was little comfort to me when I came across these snakes as I walked through the grass barefooted or as I waded in the water at the edge of the bay.

Not far from our home was the home of the Kaiser family. Mr. and Mrs. Kaiser were a kind and loving couple with a little daughter. They seemed to be a bit beyond middle age. They also appeared to be poor, because their house was somewhat run-down and their car looked rather "beaten up." They were regular in their attendance at the local Assembly of God church, which was not far away. They had wanted to adopt Vilnis, but due to their age, poverty, and religious affiliation, this was denied to them. We visited them often, however, and they seemed to want to befriend us.

We began to attend the Assembly of God church, also. There didn't seem to be any other church in the vicinity. The church building was a small white structure that had a neon cross on the outside. Inside, there were a few old benches, an electric organ, and a fan. The singing was loud and boisterous, and the people clapped their hands. One man played an accordion and another played the violin.

As a denomination, the Assemblies of God were not very old at this time. They had come into existence as a result of the Azusa Street Revival in Los Angeles that had occurred during the early part of the twentieth century. They were one of the first, if not the first, of the Pentecostal denominations.

The sanctuary of the church was usually quite warm, especially in the summer months. Therefore, several fans would be running at once and all the windows would be open. At first, this kind of demonstrative worship seemed strange to us, but we eventually got used to it and joined right in with the singing.

I have no recollection of any sermons there, but I do recall our regular Sunday school classes. I learned several hymns in that Assembly of God. Among these were "Jesus Loves Me," "When the Roll Is Called Up Yonder," "What a Friend We Have in Jesus," and "Tell Me the Story of Jesus." These were more joyous than the hymns I had learned in Germany, and I learned to like them very much. (Later in life, when I was in the parish ministry of the Lutheran church, I would play some of these same songs on the accordion along with another accordionist.)

I found that the hymns were full of meaning that I could apply to my own life. One Sunday I saw a young boy lying in a portable bed on the floor of the church. He was foaming at the mouth and was said to be "demon possessed." He was apparently unable to speak and he made strange grunts and other sounds. This was a bit scary, and I thought they would try to perform an exorcism on him. Such did not happen, though, I'm happy to report.

I understood later that Mrs. Hoikka had apologized to the Welfare Society for sending the children to this church. She explained that she felt this was better than nothing for them.

Miss Schaefer came to see us about once a week, and Mr. James Raun visited a couple of times, as well. Once, while Tolja was ill with rheumatic fever and was in the hospital, Miss Schaefer took us to the Twin Cities to see a Scout-O-Rama that was being held in a large building. We saw various kinds of exhibits there, and we were given balloons as we left.

One day Tolja had become ill and he was lying in his bed. He complained of muscle pains, especially in his legs. This caused him to be in a very unpleasant mood, and I took advantage of his situation by teasing him unfairly. (I had assumed erroneously that his condition was not as bad as he claimed it was.) I switched the lights in the bedroom on and off over and over again. This made him upset and complained about it to Anna, and she came to his rescue. I was very ashamed of myself when they took my brother to the hospital.

Before bedtime, we would engage in discussions on various subjects. Tiit claimed that he was an Estonian, although he spoke Lithuanian. He also claimed that his father was a famous hero, but I had my doubts about that assertion.

I got along best with Vilnis, but I was getting closer to Tiit. I left Karlis and Bruno alone, since they were "crybabies" and tattled regularly on others. They were also dirty fighters, even between themselves. They would pull each other's hair and kick when they were fighting.

The Hoikkas had a couple of good friends who lived on farms in the country. We visited with them a number of times. On one of these visits, I learned how to ride a tricycle and visited the circular hatchery that was filled with about 500 chicks.

On a farm of a friend of the Hoikka's

At a different farm we partook of delicious, homemade ice cream with strawberry topping. That was a yummy experience for sure. On another occasion, the Hoikkas took us to a place that had a number of rides for children, such as artificial horses moving in a circle (as in a carousel), and we were given balloons and candy. We always enjoyed these pleasurable excursions.

The older boys, Bob and Howard, left the home before we did. I believe Tiit was the first to be adopted while we were living with the Hoikkas. He spoke very enthusiastically about the fancy resort his adoptive father owned, and how he would be able to assist in its operation. His adoptive father later became the head of the Lutheran Brotherhood of the Evangelical Lutheran Church.

Jack Hoikka was a kind, hardworking man who spent a lot of his time toiling with his son at the filling station. He was middle-aged and rather haggard looking. I remember that he was very faithful about church attendance.

He would brag about the team of horses he once had, and in his spare time he would tend to the rock gardens around the house. Before I was adopted, he had come to the receiving home and he took me in an old truck to his home. We stopped along the way to visit with one of his friends and spent part of that day at a farm. Jack appeared to be failing in health, and it seemed as though financial problems were consuming him.

After Tolja and I were adopted, we learned that the Hoikkas' home had burned down and they moved to Minneapolis. Jack's health and condition had worsened and he had several strokes. He was eventually confined to bed. Anna later told us that before he died in early 1962, he had been engaged in a vigorous game of golf.

As the children were adopted one by one, any unity that our group had had was broken. The rest of us longed to be adopted, as well. I was happy to learn that I would be transferred to a different home in Minneapolis.

Anna had been very loving, generous, and patient toward us. I do not recall ever seeing her get very angry, but we knew better than to disobey her. She always kept quite busy caring for the children and elderly folks in her home. I have often marveled at her patience and ability when it came to dealing with people who were under her care.

Later Anna, in partnership with her son, Curtis, after the death of her husband, John, sold their foster-care property and established the Hoikka Nursing Home in the Twin Cities—a well-run establishment for the elderly. We visited her there several times.

A New Home

The Morrisons opened their home to us, and it was there that I came closer to a feeling of having been adopted and being a part of a family than I had ever experienced before. John Morrison was an attorney and he was away from the home a great deal of the time. However, when he was home he was always very patient and understanding toward me.

They had a young daughter who was about two years old. The Morrisons would pay me a dime for babysitting with her when they were gone. My bedroom was upstairs and I enjoyed the measure of privacy this afforded me.

On the wall in the hallway outside my room, there was a framed photograph of a young man in military uniform. Mrs. Morrison explained that it was a picture of her son who was killed during the war in a freak parachute accident. I remember that she was almost in tears as she told me about him. She expressed that it would have been more heroic if he had died in actual combat rather than as a result of an accident. However, she stressed how she wished that he had not died at all.

In a bookshelf in the hallway, I found a small booklet that discussed the process of birth. It had several illustrations that showed the fetus at several different stages. When Mrs. Morrison saw me looking through this book, she was a bit shocked. She then proceeded to tell me a little bit about the birth process, but bypassed any actual discussion of "the birds and the bees."

I began to regard this home as *my* home, and indeed it was, at least for a while. I did not mind the chores I was given, which included watering and mowing the yard, raking the leaves, and shoveling the snow. The Morrisons would usually give me a little money for each job I did. I enjoyed the family pet, which was a very friendly cocker spaniel with whom I loved to play.

Across the street was a family with a son who was older than me. This boy introduced me to the sport of soap-box racing, and I had a number of thrilling rides on these homemade carts down concrete alley slopes. He later built a fancy one for himself in which he took great pride. He gave me rides on his bicycle (I sat behind the handlebars) on his way to school. He once took me to see *The Wizard of Oz*, which was shown at the local theater.

I remember that he had a fancy erector set with an electric motor, plus other games and models of various kinds. Once, he and I took a job of mowing and raking the lawn of a neighbor. The woman paid him $1.50 plus a couple of dimes. He gave me the dimes but kept the larger sum for himself. When the woman learned of this she was furious. Soon thereafter the boy reluctantly gave me an additional fifty cents, but our relationship was forever strained after that.

Mrs. Morrison was a public school teacher, and she taught in a school that was about four blocks from our house. The school year was about to begin, so she became very busy with preparations. Once school started, I hardly got to see her. This made me wonder if I was just an extra burden for her.

I remember one time when Mrs. Morrison discussed the idea of adoption with me, but not in terms of her having a desire to adopt me, or my brother and me. She explained to me that it might be difficult to find adoptive parents who would be willing to take us both. I told her that many times Tolja and I got along better when we were apart than when we were together, so maybe it would be better for us to be adopted into separate homes. She said that that might be a good idea and assured me that everything possible was being done to find us a home.

The Morrisons gave me a Kodak Brownie camera, and this got me very interested and involved in photography.

Before school began that year, Miss Schaefer came to the home and asked me how I was getting along. I responded by saying that Mr. Morrison was gone a lot of the time and Mrs. Morrison would soon be teaching. Therefore, it might be better for me to go elsewhere.

Perhaps in response to this I was moved to the Lutheran Children's Receiving Home. I soon learned that Mr. Morrison had died of cancer. I realized that this was something they both had been dealing with for quite some time. I shall never forget Mrs. Morrison's patient efforts and loving care for me. Likewise, I will always remember Mr. Morrison's many kindnesses to me.

Personal Reflections

It is such a blessing to know that God, through Christ, has adopted us into His eternal family.

Paul wrote, "For you did not receive the spirit of bondage again to fear, but you received the Spirit of adoption by whom we cry out, 'Abba, Father'".

(ROMANS 8:15, NKJV)

CHAPTER 9

ADOPTED!

To redeem those who were under the law, that we might receive
the adoption as sons. And because you are sons, God has sent forth
the Spirit of His Son into your hearts, crying out, "Abba, Father!"
(GALATIANS 4:5–6, NKJV)

*A*bba is an Aramaic term for "father." It connotes a depth of intimacy
and love that goes beyond the word "father." A term that would be
closer to its meaning is "daddy." When you think of God as your Daddy, as
this word suggests, how does that change your perspective toward Him?

All of us who are governed by Christ have been adopted. We are now
members of the family of God. We are brothers and sisters in Christ.
When we meet together in church or elsewhere we are sharing His life
with one another.

Lutheran Children's Receiving Home

Being in a children's home had been the major part of my life experience till now, so moving to the Lutheran Children's Receiving Home
was not really new to me. However, it was a great change from living with
the Morrisons in their home. I realized that neither this home nor the

Morrisons' would be my permanent home. All the homes I had stayed in previously were temporary abodes, as well. That was just a part of my life. Permanent homes and families were for others, but not for me. However, I continued to hope that this would change one day.

Lutheran Children's Receiving Home by Como Park, St. Paul, MN, 1950

Wood working, Volodja on the right

Soon after I arrived at the Lutheran Children's Receiving Home, a German youth arrived. I remember him sitting on the stairs and weeping profusely day after day. I knew how he felt, that's for sure.

As time went on, though, he seemed to snap out of his depression and he and I were placed in the fourth grade of the Tilden School. Soon, though, he became dissatisfied with fourth grade, and he requested to be transferred to the fifth grade. This prompted me to make the same request, and I was soon with him. Our teacher was Mrs. Larson.

I did well in drawing and I remember being praised for a particular sketch I drew. It was a sketch of a girl who had posed for the class. I did not do so well in math, however. One day while Mrs. Larson was correcting papers at her desk, I was about to hand in my own paper. As I approached her desk, I noticed another student's paper, which helped me to see an oversight in one of my own answers. I hastily made a correction on my paper, and Mrs. Larson saw me doing so. She asked, "Did you cheat?" I insisted that I had not. My reasoning was that I had not copied the other student's answer outright, but had merely caught an oversight in my own answer.

Deep within, though, I knew I was not being absolutely truthful with her, but the prospect of being exposed before the entire class was too frightening to take lightly. Fortunately, she did not press the matter any further and seemed to take my word for it.

My weakest subjects have been math, calculus, algebra, chemical formulas, and physics theories. I have left those subjects for our children and grandchildren. Languages were much easier for me to master, and in college I had a double major: English and philosophy. These served me well as I prepared for the pastoral ministry. However, I praise God for those who have the genius and gifts to develop medical and technological breakthroughs, and miraculous inventions and discoveries. But don't count on me for any of that! If a job requires expertise in fields and subjects in which we are totally disqualified, let's lean on those who are qualified. Let's stick to the complementary, not competitive model for the application of our mutual gifts and talents. There should be no need for us to attempt to duplicate and viciously compete against one another.

Volodja reading on picnic table

During recesses, we were permitted to play outside, weather permitting. During rainy days we would often march to rhythmic music that was played on the phonograph in the basement. The boys in the school were eager to take part in the safety patrol. Those who did so were able to wear fancy, large badges on a white strap that went over their shoulders and had a connected waistband. Only the sixth graders were eligible for this position, however.

Different courses were taught separately. During one session of geography the students enacted a tour of the world.

Being the shortest person in the class, I did not mix in with the other students. I was very self-conscious about my height and other aspects of my appearance.

For our Christmas program the school principal asked me to take the part of Joseph in the story of the nativity. She seemed to be concerned about me and was a very cheerful and friendly person. I found a maroon bathrobe at the home, and this became my costume for the performance. My biggest problem was to control my tendency to giggle from nervousness. I must have succeeded, for I was greatly complimented for my part in the program, which simply involved my standing there.

Unfortunately, Mrs. Larson died of cancer on July 6, 1963. I shall always be very grateful to her for the way she dealt with me. She was gentle and caring. I have emulated teachers like her when working with children. I think we must always show consideration toward those who have been entrusted to us.

Though we cannot condone mischievous conduct, we must always leave a door open for every child to make amends.

Although I attended Sunday school regularly, since I had heard so many of the Bible stories before, I do not recall anything significant about our lessons there. One thing I do remember, however, is that those who had perfect attendance would receive fancy pins, which grew in length by adding new pins each year. I coveted those pins but never received any.

There was a recessed field about fifteen feet deep behind the Lutheran Children's Receiving Home. This might have been used as a small baseball field. A slide and a stairway led to the bottom. During the winter it was flooded with water and turned into a skating rink. Some adults came up with a project for the youths: to collect newspapers for recycling. After they filled a small shed and the papers went nowhere, that ended the project!

Before long I began to explore the area around the home on roller skates. I became familiar with the animals and sounds at Como Park. During Halloween we made our usual door-to-door visits and came back home with bags full of apples, candy, popcorn, and the like.

As I was coming home from school one day, a local boy stopped to ask me whether I was from another country. I replied that I was, and he encouraged me by saying that my English was good enough that it was hard for him to tell that I was from somewhere else.

Several of us would make weekly trips to the YMCA, where we would swim. We would go there by streetcar. While there, we would swim and watch cowboy movies, such as movies that starred Roy Rogers. We also saw a lot of episodes of *The Lone Ranger*. Such movies provided me with an avenue of escape from my circumstances. I remember once as I was traveling in a streetcar, I missed my stop and just kept going. I cannot recall the details, but I know I arrived home at a rather late hour.

Before Thanksgiving, an individual brought a forty-pound turkey to our home for the holiday meal, and what a delicious dinner it was. Afterward, we took turns sweeping the kitchen floor and drying the dishes.

I remember having ordered (by sending in a cereal box top) a tiny aluminum viewer with a small strip of film. It had a number of colored images on it. It was fun to look at these pictures of nature, people, and other things.

For Christmas we were taken to the home of a well-to-do rancher who showed us movies of his hunting exploits. He had several valuable hunting dogs in kennels not far from his home. While we were there, we were given presents. Mine was a simplified almanac of American figures and events, together with a weather forecast on every page.

Additional gifts were presented to us within the home itself, and they were arranged under a beautiful Christmas tree. My gift was a prized stamp album in which I would place all the stamps I had received when I was in Germany and those I had acquired since then.

Some of our counselors were Miss Johnson, Mr. Norman Lunde, and a lady named Ruth, who became the wife of Norman Lunde. Miss Johnson read bedtime stories to me quite frequently and I enjoyed these very much. Mr. Lunde came to the home a few weeks after we arrived, and it was soon evident that he "stole the show" with regard to popularity among the boys. He had an old Ford Model A, which would hardly start during the winter even though he was careful to cover the hood with a blanket each evening.

It was in this vehicle that he took us on camping trips and picnics. One time he took us to St. Peter. It was always quite an experience to ride in this car, which literally chugged along, but after a while it would usually travel at a good clip. Mr. Lunde had served in the U.S. Navy and he had many photographs of his experiences during the war. His stories and photos about World War II fascinated me so much, especially his photos of battleships. (These brought back so many memories to me.)

He collected blocks of used and unused commemorative stamps. One of his hobbies was to make blue prints of photographs on special, sensitive paper. He even allowed the older boys to practice driving his car, while explaining that before long they would be eligible to apply for a driver's license. I began to look forward to driving, as well, even though that privilege was several years away. We plunked away on his vintage Underwood typewriter and wrote notes with it to our anticipated adoptive parents.

One day Bruno happened to stop by briefly at the home. He spoke very rapidly, though, in a mixture of Latvian, German, and English (all at once). This made it very difficult and frustrating to try to communicate with him.

Miss Schaefer also came to visit me a number of times, and one time she took me shopping for clothes. I remember one shiny, blue jacket with yellow bands down the sleeves that she purchased for me. She also took us to an indoor circus that was being held somewhere in the Twin Cities. Rev. Herbert Skarie, who was with the welfare agency at the time, told us of a time when Miss Schaefer took a group of us to the city and we all had to go "wee-wee" at once. Embarrassed, she permitted us to do so at the curb of a busy downtown intersection. (We did so one by one while the others "guarded" us.)

My proudest day during this era was when I saved money and was able to purchase my own bicycle. It was a rebuilt black J.C. Higgins bike with a light that was powered by a wheel-rim driven generator on the rear wheel. There was a loud-sounding bell on the handlebars, solid fenders, and good reflectors. I was very proud of my new bicycle, which I considered to be a true luxury. (It cost me $75.00!) Many of the children desired to have bikes, but they could not afford them. The bikes at the home were in need of repair, and we were afraid to take them very far, for fear that they would break down.

J.C. Higgins Bicycle, 1950

It took me a few days to get the hang of riding my new bike, but I eventually did, and neither the bike nor I were injured in the process. My new prized possession served me well at the home and after I was adopted. I was so proud of it.

How did I save enough money to acquire a bicycle? It was because I was very frugal with any money I received. My average allowance was seventy-five cents a week. The other kids wanted me to spend my money, but I would save it instead of buying comic books, candy, and going to the movies. When I decided to spend it, I made sure it was for something that I dearly wanted.

While I was at the Lutheran Receiving Home, Tolja was staying with the Gustafsons. I would visit him on several weekends there. When returning home from one of these visits, I again went too far on a streetcar. I had gotten lost and Mrs. Gustafson had to notify the police. They found me and transported me back to the receiving home.

I also visited Tolja in the hospital once and played a game of checkers with him. A press photographer was there and he took a picture of us that was later published in the *Minneapolis Tribune* and *Minneapolis Daily Star*. The article stated that Tolja was better at checkers than Volodja! (This was certainly true.)

In my mind, I could not "set down roots" until I knew I had a more-permanent home. Everything in my life up to this time had been transitory. Now I was looking for something more lasting and fulfilling. I wondered what it would be like to have one's own father and mother, and to live with a family in a home. I wanted to be loved and to have some semblance of a normal life. I no longer wanted to be a "nomad."

The moment I had been waiting for finally came during the Easter season of 1950. Mr. and Mrs. Boe had expressed an interest in adopting us, and we were ultimately adopted by them on June 17 of that same year. When Mr. Boe came to the home, I was eager to discover what kind of car he was driving, so I ran outside to see. It was a dark-blue 1946 Pontiac. It did not seem to be the automobile of a very rich man, I thought.

I could sense that Mr. and Mrs. Boe were concerned about the first impression they would make on me and my brother. When they came into the lobby, I literally badgered them with questions while Tolja ran around the building, seemingly unconcerned.

For a few months we corresponded with Mr. and Mrs. Boe, and I was pleased to see positive responses from them in their letters; they came back for several visits. During one of our visits with our prospective parents we went by elevator to the top of the largest building in Minneapolis, the Foshay Tower. Today, of course, it is small compared to much-higher buildings, including the IDS skyscraper. We went to a restaurant that served us French fries—a delicious food that I had neither seen nor eaten before. I called them "French flies" and everyone laughed at my mispronunciation. In future eat-outs, when I had French fries, I would use the mispronunciation again, and I always had a response of laughter from the others. Even today, my grandchildren laugh at this.

Here is one of the letters we wrote to Mr. and Mrs. Boe in May or early June of 1950, just prior to our adoption.

Dear Mr. and Mrs. Boe:

WE ARE VERY GLAD THAT YOU WROTE US LETTERS. We hope that when we go to Moorhead we wuld [sic] be wery [sic] happy. Tolja dosent [sic] get angry so fast since he came home. We heard about that boat you bought. We are thinking about all the fun we are going to have in the lake. We are waiting for you to comer [sic] and get us for a nice ride. A week ago went on a camping trip. We stayed there two nights. I caught two bullheads. We where [sic] near Lake Crystal, about one hundred miles from the Home. We borrowed three boats, for fishing.

We are studying about conservation, in school. There are five groups; wild life, forests, human, minerals and water and soil. I am in the group that is working on forest conservation. People are coming to see what we have done, next Monday evening.

Good-bye! We will see you when you come to pick us up. We will be ready for you.

Your friends,
Tolja and Volodja

Volodja and Tolja

Tolja with dog

Volodja with dog

During the Easter season we went with the Boes to Kabekona Lake for a time of fellowship. I was beginning to feel as if I was becoming a part of their family, but at the same time, I was afraid that they might lose interest in us. Our initial visits in their home were joyful and exciting. It was thrilling to see how quickly this progress toward family membership was developing.

Life with My New Family

I believe it was the last day of school when Mr. and Mrs. Boe came to visit us again. I actually encountered Mr. Boe on my way home from school. The sense of joy I had at seeing him can hardly be described. When we eventually departed from the Lutheran Receiving Home, various counselors gave us their farewell wishes and took pictures of us on the front steps. Mr. and Mrs. Boe also took a picture of us as we pulled apart a chicken wishbone on the front porch. I remember making a wish that our adoption would go through and that all would be well.

Tolja and Volodja Sinegins pulling wishbone prior to adoption
by Rev. and Mrs. (Hilda) Victor C. Boe at Lutheran
Children's Receiving Home, St. Paul, MN, June, 1950

My future father served as men's dormitory resident head of Brown Hall at Concordia College. Mr. and Mrs. Boe resided at one end of the building in an apartment. He had constructed green-painted, individual beds for us on the opposite sides of our bedroom. Tolja and I were "forced" to learn to live together once again. It was not easy for us to do so, however, due to our competitive natures. We would get into brawls and fights from time to time, which was simply sibling rivalry, a normal part of growing up. However, once, when my father came home from work, he found us fighting on the floor, and this had resulted in my having a bloody nose. He was quick to end the fight, and we soon forgot all about it.

Adoption, 1950

THE CONCORDIAN – Concordia College; Moorhead, MN – Feb. 23, 1973 – featuring Rev./Dean of Students VICTOR BOE & FAMILY upon his retirement, covering span of near 50 years as student & staff member at CC.

"I was in Montana in 1950, I recall . . . and my wife called and said that . . . "Lutheran Welfare in Minneapolis . . . thinks that they have two boys for us.

"We never dreamt of taking two at a time, but these two fellows were brothers (war orphans from Latvia) and the decision was that it would be better if they could be together . . . and so we tackled the assignment. It wasn't always easy and the boys recognize that now. They raise the question frequently, 'How could you do it?'

"They are both pastors now. The older one graduated here and went to Wartburg Seminary in Iowa . . . and became a missionary in Nigeria. The other boy . . . was a freshman at Concordia . . . and (went into the Marines). He . . . finished Concordia and went to Luther Seminary.

"The oldest is at Faith Lutheran in Bismarck . . . the youngest is a pastor at Echo, Minn. . . .

"We have four grandchildren . . . So both boys are very happy, with their lovely wives and the best we could wish for them."

Same photo, featured in "The Concordian"

I avoided fighting with Tom afterward, even when he prodded me to do so prior to his enlisting in the U.S. Marine Corps. I stuck with academics, which served my schooling needs well.

Fortunately, our activities in school served to distract us. Tolja's superior strength was enough to keep me from ever provoking him. We continued to compete in different ways. He usually beat me at chess. Yes, he was a very intelligent individual. There were a few times when Tolja came to my defense when others were attempting to bully me, and I am so grateful for him doing so on those occasions.

The fact is we complemented each other in various respects. As I said before, he had an outgoing personality while I was shy and bashful. He was eager to make pals among his schoolmates and neighbors; I was not. I was withdrawn, contemplative.

While we were living in the dormitory, I delivered the *Minneapolis Morning Tribune* to many students and faculty members. This served as a source of some spending money for me, as well as an avenue for building relationships with others.

Also while living in the dormitory, Tolja and I decided to choose new names. He picked Thomas Christopher and I chose Peter Volodja.

Shortly after adoption, 1950, Brown Hall, Concordia College,
Moorhead, MN June 1950

We all eventually moved into a newly built house in Moorhead. I enjoyed helping our dad lay the lower-level floor. We also enjoyed our Minnesota lake home at Kabekona Lake and spent much time searching the woods for berries and the lakeshore for agates. We had many fishing trips and pontoon rides and enjoyed many lakeshore friends. That area of Kabekona Lake was called "Preacher's Point" because many pastors and their families vacationed there.

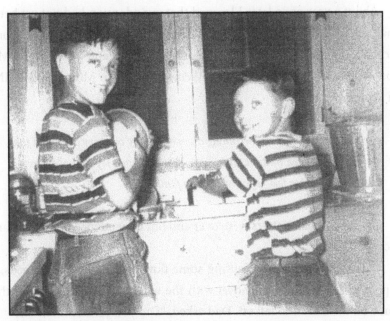

At Kabekona Lake, early 1950s

During our high school years Tolja attended a Lutheran school (Oak Grove Lutheran Academy in Fargo, North Dakota) while I attended a public school in Moorhead, Minnesota. He joked, "I am going to Heaven; you are going to hell." Of course, I never believed that. Eventually, we both became Lutheran pastors!

It was most enjoyable to meet my new relatives, especially the Eversons, and grandparents, uncles, aunts, and several cousins and their relations. Soon Mr. and Mrs. Boe became "Father" and "Mother" to us. A bit later we started calling him "Daddy," and eventually "Dad," but I always called Mrs. Boe "Mother."

My father eventually became the dean of men at Concordia College, and my mother was a librarian there. The Concordia College newspaper, *The Concordian*, described the adoption of Tolja and Volodja in these words in the April 28, 1950 publication: "There will be no dearth of activity in the Boe mansion from now on. The boys are made of self-winding coiled springs, and are on the go all day long. They like to eat ice cream, cake, and chicken. ('Gonna have chik-kan, yes?')"

About a year or so later I learned that our adoption had not yet been finalized, and this caused me great concern. I let Dad know how concerned I was. He told me that these things take time, and he was right. Mr. Boe wrote a letter to the Lutheran Welfare Society in Minneapolis, MN, on September 14, 1951:

We feel that the boys are becoming more and more our very own, and the feeling seems to be mutual. They have brought much joy and pleasure to our home, and we feel very much like a family.

Later, the legal matters were over and our dependence on the welfare society had ended.

One day when I was planting some flowers and chopping weeds, I happened to drive over a shovel with the wheelbarrow. This caused the spade on the shovel to fall off. Dad asked, "Did you break the shovel?

I said, "No, I cannot remember doing that."

He became fuming mad and said, "I ask you again, did you break the shovel?"

I said, "I know that I drove over it, but I did not notice the blade coming off."

At that he exploded and said some coarse things that might have burned out the insides of many young children, because his wrath was so scorching. I realized that he would have said these things to me had I been his blood-born son. Adoption had nothing to do with it. It was within his nature to "blow up" like that. When Dad cooled off, he confessed to having temper flare-ups that were rooted in childhood traumas, and he duly apologized.

We can express anger without being rabidly angry. (See Ephesians 4:26.) We must not let the sun go down upon our wrath, and learn to release our anger without sinning. We can use the energy that is generated by our anger to mow the lawn, take a walk, or use our talents in a productive way. We must not abuse or hurt a loved one.

On the cross Jesus said, "Father, forgive them, for they do not know what they do".

(LUKE 23:34, NKJV)

To this extent, our reciprocal adoption relationship in Christ was intact and complete. It could not have been better even if we had been related by blood. We must remember, however, that this firm bond is possible only through Christ. There can be no hope outside of His love and way.

During the summer months my brother and I attended the Moorhead State Teachers' College Laboratory School. I enjoyed my time there because it was relatively free from scholastic tension. It was here where I began to make some friends. Two of my friends were David Dussere and Cordell Krabbenhoft.

My teachers during my sixth and seventh grades were very attentive and kind. These teachers, though, were only teaching part-time, and each of them had their own way of doing things. I greatly respected such teachers as Mr. Ursin in shop and Mr. Brand in math. I admired our history teacher, Miss Solem, who knew history "from pins to pyramids," as she would say.

My hope was to go on to college, so I decided to attend the junior high school where academic competition would be keen, making my preparation for college more effective. I joined the band (in the clarinet section) under Mr. Buslee, and I sang with the glee club under Miss Newton. I took one year of piano lessons and quickly learned how to play the instrument, along with the organ and pipe organ. I also taught myself how to play the trumpet. To this day, that song I learned early on continues to ring in my memory—"Marlene." I enjoyed the courses I took and appreciated the trust and support of our principal, Mr. Closter.

There were the usual bullies in the school, however, and they tried to get the best of me—without success. Like a student who had bullied me in the former school, there was a tall bully in junior high school, as well. He pushed me around and one day asked me if he could borrow my bicycle for a few minutes. He said he would give me a nickel if I let him do so. Reluctantly, I agreed and was thrilled to get my bike back awhile later.

Another tall fellow took after me as I fled atop the Concordia College bleachers during a football game. He had heard that I had "squealed" on a student for breaking the seat boards by swinging on them. The student who had broken the seat boards resented me for reporting him, and his punishment was to pay for new seat boards. He remained somewhat hostile toward me until the afternoon when I gave him a nickel.

Another time, after a gym class, a lad who was about my size challenged me to a fight. He thought I was a coward and that I would run away from him. He was surprised, however, when I took him up on his challenge and agreed to meet him after school on the lawn of another student's family that was near the Moorhead Junior High School. He did not show up for the fight! His explanation was that he had to go home to change his clothes.

I took one year of tumbling, under the direction of my physical education instructor, Mr. Hanson. I gave this up, though, after I landed on my head without hand support and chipped my tooth during a leap-and-somersault stunt involving jumping over an obstacle.

Once I got to senior high, Shocky Strand of the athletics department tried to get me to go out for wrestling, but I found that my leg and pelvic joints would get easily dislocated whenever I engaged in such activity, and the pain from this was very intense. It seemed better for me to continue with band and orchestra instead.

I also participated in speech contests. The most notable of these was the Voice of Democracy contest. I competed in several of these and won various medals and prizes. My interests pointed me more and more in an intellectual and spiritual direction. I began to explore and examine spiritual dynamics and the foundations of faith. The seed of the Spirit that Mrs. Yeats had sown in me when I was in Germany was now beginning to take root and blossom forth as I took steps toward a relationship with Christ.

For two years I worked at Ted Hornbacher's Super Valu Store. There I carried out groceries to customers' cars and I bagged produce. During the summer of 1956, I worked for the U.S. Forestry Service by pulling wild currant and gooseberry bushes among the white pines in the Potlatch timber country near Bovill, Idaho. We stayed in an abandoned logging camp that had a solid log bunkhouse.

During the summer of 1957, I worked at the Hotel Powers parking lot in Fargo, North Dakota. While I was there I saw a tornado rip through the town and devastate a good part of the city. This massive, roaring funnel left eleven people dead.

From each of these jobs I learned about life's responsibilities and relationships with others. I learned to be frugal and careful. I was becoming an adult.

My interest in knowing how things tick did not diminish during this time. I needed to know the how and why of things, so I would tear into discarded radios, watches, electrical gadgets of all sorts, and other objects that ignited my curiosity. By now, though, I was able to repair some of these items and had accumulated a box full of bolts, nuts, screws, nails, wires, and brass and copper objects, which allowed me to refurbish and even make things.

Even while I was in college I found very few things more stimulating than being able to tear into things, especially those that had been abandoned by the college physics department. By the end of college, though, my interest in mechanical things had been satisfied, and my new interest was to become deeply and seriously engaged in the examination of human relationships, philosophy, and even theology.

How are relationships formed? What dynamics are involved? Why is it easier to relate to some people and not others? What is the meaning of love? Why do some relationships fall apart?

The very happy relationships I experienced among the Boe family members and friends provided me with answers to some of these important questions. They were also the starting point for looking into the unhappy and demonic side of life. Why are some people likable while others are not? Sometimes it seems impossible to get close to some people. Why is this?

My inquiring mind caused me to look for how relationships worked in a way that was similar to how I would try to see how certain mechanical objects worked. These are some of the questions I now sought to find answers for, but the overarching question regarding relationships was, "What does it mean to be in Christ?" This led me to explore a related question: "What is the difference between those who believe in Him and those who don't?" How can one tell whether or not a person who calls himself a Christian is actually a Christian at heart? How can one tell whether or not a person who does not claim to be a Christian might actually be a disciple of the Lord?

I had already learned that there were at least two entirely different worlds of relationships within which people were living or were capable of living in. As I began to find answers to some of these questions and several others, I began to consider the possibility of becoming a minister of the Gospel. My thinking went in this direction: either there was something "to it"—this matter of a personal relationship with Jesus Christ—or it was an innocent bluff that was designed to keep children nice and obedient.

Because there was no certainty as to whether or not I had been baptized, the pastor of Trinity Lutheran Church in Moorhead, Minnesota, baptized me on January 10, 1954. Later that year, on May 23, 1954, I was confirmed as a member of the church. I remember that I was a bit nervous during the baptism and feared that I might burst out in laughter. I also wondered as I was being baptized if God would somehow make a special appearance, but nothing unusual happened, which was both a relief and a disappointment at the same time.

Personal Reflections

The next part of this book deals with the steps that led me to become a Lutheran pastor. My "great awakening" came during the 1960–1961 school year at Concordia College. I had graduated from Moorhead Senior High School in the spring of 1957. (It was significant to me that I graduated in the top 10 percent of my class.)

I became a naturalized citizen of the United States on June 25, 1957, and I attended Concordia College, from which I graduated on May 29, 1961, with a B.A. degree. I graduated cum laude. I had a double major in English and philosophy. During my freshman year in college I won the Freedom Shrine speech contest that was sponsored by the Junior Chamber of Commerce in Moorhead. My interest in public speaking continued, as did my interest in music. I also had tried my hand at art and painting. All of these activities were somewhat amateurish, but they gave me a sense of identity and purpose.

The next chapter deals with some of my spiritual history and how I came to know the way of Christ, not as an intellectual exercise but as a live, interpersonal relationship between Christians or persons empowered by God's love and spirit. Words can neither define nor capture this relationship; it must be experienced to know it.

CHAPTER 10

CHRIST IS AT MY HELM

God is Spirit, and those who worship Him
must worship in spirit and truth.
(JOHN 4:24, NKJV)

A Regimen of Reading

Mr. McLaughlin was my tenth-grade biology instructor, and from him I learned that the conception of children requires the physical participation of a man. Previously I had believed that children were conceived spontaneously in the wombs of their mothers! If the children looked like their fathers, I felt it was due possibly to some magnetic attraction and influence the husband had upon his wife.

One day in class I asked Mr. McLaughlin, "How long does it take for a father to be with the mother until the baby begins to look like the father?"

He answered, "Why, no time at all." It was obvious that he was somewhat embarrassed both by my question and the answer he gave. The members of the class chuckled while I wondered what I had said that was wrong.

After the class, Mr. McLaughlin showed me a film about the genital functions of pigs. The movie did not show anything about copulation, however, and so I felt that my question had not been truly addressed.

On that day when I went home after school I asked my father about this. He seemed to feel at a loss as to how to approach the subject with me. I spared him the need to say more, and began to read books of all sorts—hundreds of them, and they provided me with many answers about life and human nature.

Some of the books I read were *Out of the Depths* by Anton Boisen, and numerous books by Soren Kierkegaard, Dr. William E. Hulme (a seminary professor), Carroll A. Wise, Dr. Paul Tournier, and Dr. Stewart Hiltner. Two books that were especially important to me were *Spiritual Therapy* by Young and Meiburg and *Depth Psychology and Salvation* by Wilfried Daim.

In addition, I read many books about the Bible, English, science, philosophy, art, theology, exegesis, linguistics (including English, Latin, German, Greek, Hebrew, and Aramaic). While I was in college I strongly considered going into the medical profession; I had a great interest in biology, anatomy, astronomy, geology, atomic structures, and other scientific subjects. I wanted to become a pediatrician, but my lack of talent in chemistry, math, and related subjects put an end to that.

However, gradually my field of interest began to narrow somewhat. I was becoming very interested in interpersonal relationships as a field of study. I was delighted to discover that current writings coincided quite strongly with my own experiences and conclusions. Eventually I went to Wartburg Seminary where everything seemed to come together for me.

Reading is so helpful when one is growing up. Books open doors that will remain closed if a child does not read. Books are more than an escape; they are a way of finding oneself in a very confusing world.

Peaks, Plateaus, and Depressions

During my senior year in high school I voluntarily submitted a brief thesis to my English instructor, Miss Lydia Busles. The topic of my thesis was emotional peaks, plateaus, and depressions. She seemed very pleased with my work, and this propelled me into further exploration into these topics.

I realized that somewhere in all of this lay the clue as to why some people become raving maniacs under certain conditions while others remain stable and loving under the same conditions. I knew, also, that through this investigation I would find the significance of the cross of Jesus Christ for my life and the lives of others. I already knew that His cross is a stumbling block to the faithless and the spiritually blind, but I did not truly know Him and His way. I wanted to, though, but how was the question.

I needed to find the root of human nature, and I had quite a bit of help along the way. The trust and understanding of my religion instructor, Rev. Arthur H. Grimstad, my father, and Rev. Oscar A. Anderson were greatly instrumental in helping me find direction for my life. Had it not been for them, who knows what course in life I would have pursued? Something that also helped me at that time was a poem I wrote:

A soul in body and in mind,
Not knowing where to go—
Sometimes seeing the glory of the Lord,
But more often traveling blind.

Body and soul and mind—all three,
Acting together as one...
The soul regretting what had been done
When the others become but debris.

It is not within my realm
To shed these ancestral blinds.
But victory I can be sure to find,
Because Christ is at my helm.

I thank God that I had the opportunity to teach sixth-grade Sunday school pupils at Trinity Lutheran Church from 1957–1959, for as I taught, I sensed the very presence of Jesus. He was drawing and bonding us together.

Richard Johnson, who was a premedical student at Concordia and a member of the Athenian Society, to which I also belonged, asked whether I might be interested in working as a counselor at the Metigoshe Scout Reservation in Bottineau, North Dakota. This seemed to be the right thing for me to do, so I accepted his invitation with joy and enthusiasm.

The summers of 1958, 1959, and 1960 at Metigoshe were very rewarding and joyful for me. The enthusiasm and acceptance I received from the scouts and scoutmasters were tremendous. I spent nearly thirty years thereafter involved with the scouting program. I had similar experiences teaching Sunday school, and serving as a counselor at Bible camps and, later, in Nigeria, West Africa.

During the first summer at Metigoshe I taught nature, pioneering, knife and axe, compass, and cooking. The next summer I taught primarily nature and pioneering. During the third summer I was the program director, and I helped to schedule the various events throughout the two weeks of camp. It was a great joy for me to play the field pump organ for worship services and to assist the scouts in flag-raising and flag-lowering. I particularly recall the numerous and joyful campfire sessions.

One of my greatest joys in life was working with children and young people, and in the summer of 1962, I returned to Metigoshe to serve as chaplain of the scout camp. During those weeks my positive and joyful experience was strengthened; I was so happy to serve in this capacity. My relationship with the scouts was solidified and was greatly rewarding to me, as was my developing relationship with Jesus Christ.

Personal Reflections

I can say with assurance that there has never been a single day in my life for which I was not grateful and thankful before God. As I said before, a God-consciousness was part of my life from the early days. We must always remember that our severest trials and hardships in life can serve to strengthen our unity in Christ and can be seen as avenues of blessings through Him.

One thing that equaled or surpassed my summers at Metigoshe was sharing with more than eighty young people at a week of worship and fun at the Lutheran Bible Camp in the Absarokee Mountains in Montana. That took place in the summer of 1964. I also had the opportunity to share the Word of God at Our Redeemer's Lutheran Church to over 600 souls in two morning services and an evening banquet.

I was beginning to find my niche in life. I loved to preach, teach, and counsel with others. All of these experiences seemed to confirm my calling, and I began to grow eager to be a full-fledged pastor, as my father had been.

CHAPTER 11

WALKING THROUGH OPEN DOORS

Closing Summary Account about Peter Volodja (Sinegins) Boe

As I approached graduation from Wartburg Theological Seminary in Dubuque, Iowa, in May of 1965, Rev. Donald Wahlgren informed me of a great opportunity. He served as chaplain of the Numan Teacher Training College in Numan, Nigeria, West Africa, and notified me that his position was currently vacant. I applied for it and was accepted through our American Lutheran Church World Missions' lead spokesperson, the Rev. Theodore Paul Fricke and the Rev. Lowell H. Hesterman, ALC Spokesman for African Missions. I was duly ordained as pastor and commissioned as a missionary on June 6, 1965, at Trinity Lutheran Church in Moorhead, Minnesota, on Pentecost Sunday. Rev. Victor C. Boe, my father, was among the participants as ordinator.

May 26, 1965, Graduation from Wartburg Seminary, Dubuque, IA

Vic and Hilda Boe after Ordination and Commissioning service

That fall I departed for Nigeria, West Africa, settling at Numan, Sudan United Mission (Danish), Nigeria. I served as teacher of English, Bible knowledge, and principles of education at the Bronnum Secondary School and the Numan Teacher Training College in Northern Nigeria, West Africa, from 1965–1971. During that time I also preached at the Numan church, played my accordion for singing, served among the children, and wrote photo-accompanied articles for *The Missionary* magazine. My main form of transport was a sleek, smooth-running Honda motorcycle, which enabled me to drive over narrow, sandy, and hilly roads and terrain. One such journey included a trek to a village to witness and photo-document the initiation into manhood of young boys of the *Bille* tribe—nearly sixty—and also of the *N'Torong* tribe, an event published in *The Nigeria Magazine* in two issues in 1968.

Nigeria

Tribal chiefs, Nigeria

Church in Nigeria

Group of Bille candidates relaxing after the 'March of Death' with the author posing with them

a herd of buffalo stampeding toward Bille. When Manasseh at first pointed them out to me, I could hardly believe my eyes. It seemed that this large crowd was dancing in one place, not far from Bille. But as we got closer to it, it was apparent that it was moving slowly, chanting and dancing, toward Bille, to join with the Bille throng and candidates. Two lines of men and older youths were holding sticks (whips) in their hands; one man was holding an old gun up in his hand. All in all, it was a far more energetic crowd than the Bille crowd. Mr Manasseh kept saying: 'See how perfectly they dance. They are doing it the correct way. They are doing it much better than the Bille people are doing it. They are following the tradition correctly,

while the Bille people are more and more departing from our ancient traditions. Watch closely how the N'torong people do it.' The dress and appearance of the N'torong candidates was not very distinguishable from that of the Bille youths, however, although their dancing rhythm was much more lively, the candidates accenting, the rhythm with their foot jingles and two groups of people chanting alternately. The next day they chanted in unison the phrase.

"*Wo—woye!*"/rest/rest/"*Wo—woye!*"/rest/rest; or step/step, etc. (Notes with beat value: start on staff and go down—A2/Q3-C3+/rest/rest. . .)

But no sooner had the N'torong crowd reached the edge of the Bille compounds than its stick-

Bille candidates, Nigeria

181

I met Betty while I was on furlough (1967–1969). I earned my MA degree in English during that time at the College of St. Thomas in St. Paul, Minnesota. During my last two years in Nigeria, Betty and I exchanged letters. We had made no commitments. I sent her an engagement ring from Nigeria and returned to the States in the fall of 1971. We were married on December 18, 1971. Owing to a trend of expatriates departing to permit nationals to take over operations, teaching, and pulpits, I remained in the States and went on to serve parishes in Minnesota, North Dakota, and Iowa for many years.

God has blessed us with four fantastic children—three sons and a daughter—and twelve remarkable grandchildren. We could not be better blessed! What a joy it is to be a part of a close-knit family in Jesus Christ and to be a pastor/minister within His one Church, home, and eternal family!

INSIGHTS AND
SCRIPTURES

1. All basic knowledge relevant to salvation is found in the Bible. We must read and study the Scriptures—both Old and New Testaments—because they reinforce each other.

2. What is written by the Spirit of God in Christ is understandable only by the same Spirit. Words by themselves are not divine but can be used in a negative way. *The letter kills, but the Spirit gives life* (2 Corinthians 3:6, NKJV).

3. We are able to love one another in Christ, because God through Christ loved us first. *This is My commandment, that you love one another as I have loved you. Greater love has no one than this, than to lay down one's life for his friends* (John 15:12–13, NKJV).

4. *For where two or three are gathered together in My* name [Spirit, love, Word], *I am there in the midst of them"* (Matthew 18:20, NKJV). This can be anywhere, at any time.

5. God does not hold us accountable for what we do not know. (See James 4:17, John 9:41, and John 15:22–24.) We reveal the living presence of Christ to all around us.

6. Christians do not see each other as black or white, infant or adult, male or female, rich or poor, or weak or powerful, but we see all as being equally important within the family of Christ. Many parts, one body, but all parts are equally important. (See 1 Corinthians 12.)

7. It is important to exercise extreme caution in what you say and do, because those outside of the Christian fold may turn against you. Any slight prejudice on your part will negate the power of Christ's love and Spirit. (See Acts 10:1ff.) Peter regarded Cornelius as "unclean," but verse 34 goes on to say that "...*God shows no partiality.*" Jesus saw the cross before Him. Be prepared to bear your cross of responsibility in the path of Jesus Christ.

8. Reading the scriptures enables us to graduate from milk to solid food. *For everyone who partakes only of milk is unskilled in the word of righteousness, for he* [she] *is a babe* [carnal; slave of impulses of human nature]. *But solid food belongs to those who are of full age...*" (Hebrews 5:13–14, NKJV). Jesus knew all that, of course, and almost always spoke to the crowds in parables. *All these things Jesus spoke to the multitude in parables; and without a parable He did not speak to them...*" (Matthew 13:34, NKJV).

9. *"Behold... I will make a new covenant with the house of Israel... I will put My law in their minds, and write it on their hearts... they all shall know Me, from the least of them to the greatest...*" (Jeremiah 31:31–34, NKJV). (See also Hebrews 8:8–12.) That time is now. There are many versions of "Christ" and "Christianity" out there in the world around you. Many of these are a variation of the "feel-good gospel"—no cross, no pain, no personal inconvenience, no discomfort—custom-made to your personal satisfaction, thrill, and enjoyment—just what you want! This is faux/pseudo Christianity. *Many will say to Me in that day, 'Lord, Lord, have we not prophesied in Your name, cast out demons in Your name, and done many wonders in Your name?' And then I will declare to them, 'I never knew you; depart from Me, you who practice lawlessness!'* (Matthew 7:22–23, NKJV).

10. Our knowledge of God's law and of the way of Christ might be composed within a few paragraphs, but interpreting His law and the way of Christ into every conceivable this-life situation is near nigh humanly impossible. No book, not even the Scriptures, can spell out everything about everything. However, you may have access to knowledge that is not available to anyone else, so be sure to share it.

11. We are all differently gifted. In the way of Christ, we do not compete against one another, but we complement one another. Our goal should be to foster togetherness.

12. None of us can say or write everything about everything. Attempts have been made to do just that. The Ten Commandments became the Mishnah; the Mishnah became the Talmud—a massive encyclopedia relevant to its time but rendered quickly obsolete by the passage of time. (Even the Scriptures have to be linguistically updated.) Be sure to read and study the Scriptures as regularly as possible. Commit as many Scripture passages as possible to memory. Record all the insights that are revealed to you by the Spirit of Christ. Be soundly rooted in the Scriptures, which are read and studied by multitudes around the globe.

13. Let's not lament, mourn, or brood for even an instant over our sins, imperfections, failures, etc., which may be too many to count. Rather, let our primary focus always be on the perfection that Christ creates with and among us—making us brilliant, beautiful, and glorious in His and each other's sight. In this way we will be able to overpower the greatest addiction of mankind: the worship of the three-headed monster of Me, Myself, and I.

14. Likely the greatest killer of mankind is people falling into depression and feeling sorry for themselves. The resulting sense of hopelessness and total unworthiness brings about the total absence of the very will to live, the desire to be alive. The only antidote to this is the Spirit-empowered path and the love-bonding of Christ. Our challenge is that none of us owns a guaranteed method for converting a single soul to the way of Christ. Christ accomplishes this through us according to His timing and initiative.

15. For us, the Word, love, and commands of God in Christ are clear and obvious. But as soon as we translate His unchangeable, eternal Word into visible words, symbols, and objects, they immediately become targets of deliberate attacks and misuse. Remember, Satan used Scripture during the temptations of Jesus in the wilderness. No words, in and of themselves, are holy. Be alert to know how persons use and misuse words. For us, a

Christ-governed conscience compels us to select only words and actions that conform to His love and will.

16. If Christ is not our Savior at our very weakest point, He is not our Savior at all! If you are saying to yourself, "Oh, but I try so hard to be perfect, yet I fail over and over again," you have not surrendered yourself totally to His will. When you permit yourself to be directed and guided by His will, Word, and law, sin no longer clouds your vision of His glory, light, and power. You have become part of His Easter victory and glory—a new self that is liberated and freed from the shackles of sin and the fear of death. Forever! *Therefore, if anyone is in Christ, he is a new creation; old things have passed away; behold, all things have become new"* (2 Corinthians 5:17, NKJV). (See also Ephesians 2:13ff.) *"that you put off, concerning your former conduct, the old man which grows corrupt according to the deceitful lusts, and be renewed in the spirit of your mind, and that you put on the new man which was created according to God, in true righteousness and holiness"* (Ephesians 4:22–24, NKJV).

17. *Woe to you, scribes and Pharisees, hypocrites! For you travel land and sea to win one proselyte, and when he is won, you make him twice as much a son of hell as yourselves* (Matthew 23:15, NKJV). False motivation for "church growth" too often drives "membership drives" in churches and other groups. The qualifications for this are based on financial donations, social status, and appearances. *And the King will answer and say to them, 'Assuredly, I say to you, inasmuch as you did it to one of the least of these My brethren, you did it to Me'* (Matthew 25:40, NKJV).

18. When referring to the ministry of Christ, say, "God through Christ did that, performed miracles, accomplished all—not Jesus by His own will, ambition, and initiative." Jesus never claimed any credit for self!

19. When we come to an unproductive "dead end" in life and our formula for forward movement and progress in life fizzles out, we may have to call upon God in Christ to "reinvent" us, equip us with brand-new armor, reinspired initiative, and foresight. Some prophets have done that. Whatever the Lord calls us to do, He will supply the means and the way. I have passed the age

of eighty by placing my primary focus on the way, the path, the will, and the love of Jesus Christ.

20. A popular self-delusion goes like this: "If I do good things ninety-nine percent of the time, and secretly do the opposite one percent of the time, God will forgive it and forget it. After all, no one is perfect. We are all equally sinners." *For there is no difference; for all have sinned and fall short of the glory of God* (Romans 3:22b–23, NKJV). This self-justifying notion misuses scriptures. The Way of Christ demands all or none. If the Way of Christ is not our salvation at our very weakest point, it is not our salvation at all. None! We are living in a world of total self-deception. Rather, let us focus our primary attention on the new life that God has created for us through Christ's death and resurrection!

21. When Rose Austrums was asked, "Do you believe in Jesus Christ as your Lord and Savior?" she replied, "According to what church group or denomination?" Her personal example of self-denial and commitment to the 130 little ones really declared the answer loud and clear. Again, "...*Inasmuch as you did it to one of the least of these My brethren, you did it to me*" (Matthew 25:40, NKJV). She was raised a Baptist and had seen the abuse of "church" power in Latvia by German barons and landlords. She saw more meaning in the native beliefs of the land than in imported and imposed creeds and rituals. These native beliefs followed the *Dievturi* movement. In the last few years of her life, her heart was turned to Jesus Christ. Perhaps there are some among Jewish and other brethren for whom "Christ," "Church," and "Christianity" have become so politicized and misused as to evoke no reverence, honor, or respect—only contempt, derision, and scorn. Similar labels of "Jew" and "Jewish," even in the form of yellow cloth stars, brought scorn, abuse, and death to millions during World War II. Would terms such as "universal/divine conscience" work better, and point to the existence and presence of globally- and universally-recognized universal law and justice? May our prayer be that we can work together toward peace and integration, breaking down walls of prejudice, conceit, and pride. The opposite of recognizing a central, unifying

authority and power is the worship of self. Human nature is the same animal in all of us, with its ups, downs, and variations.

22. We cannot write or say everything about everything. (See John 21:25.) Even the Scriptures do not claim to say everything about everything. Paul was aware of that and he said, "...*Work out your own salvation with fear and trembling...*" (Philippians 2:12, NKJV). Your insights are so important. Share them, starting here, and then reflect upon them:

_____

_____

_____

_____

PUBLICATIONS BY AND
ABOUT PETER BOE

A poem published prior to graduation from college in the student newspaper:

> O little child, thou knowest not
> That in thy footsteps I do trod.
> Whene'r your lips with joy expand,
> My heart, too, blossoms out of hand.
>
> So do not fear my outstretched arms
> Nor reject my gestures filled with charms.
> For we have a Father true and one,
> We are His children, born from above.

The Voice and Image of God. Wartburg Seminary, Dubuque, Iowa, 1962.

Reflections. Wartburg Seminary, Dubuque, Iowa, April 1965.

The Missionary Magazine of the American Lutheran Church, photo-accompanied articles, 1965–1971.

The Rites of Manhood in the Bille Tribe.
> *Nigeria Magazine*, September/November and December issues, 1969.
> *Practical Anthropology*, January–February 1971.

Woodbury County History, Woodbury County Genealogical Society, 1984; pp. 200–201.

Survivors' List. National Holocaust Museum, Washington, D.C. Museum was dedicated in 1993.

A Universal/International Guide for Christian Leaders on Identity and Mission, February 7, 1997.

Insights at 80, Compiled 9/13/17 – 10/16/17.

"Pastor Recalls Being Saved from Nazis as an Orphan," *The Sioux City Journal,* Friday, March 2, 2018. Article written by Mason Dockter. Photo by Tym Hynds.

"A Jewish-born orphan becomes a Lutheran pastor," *Living Lutheran* magazine of the Evangelical Lutheran Church in America, July 2018, pp. 24–26. Article written by Jeff Favre. Photo by Tym Hynds.

www.ingramcontent.com/pod-product-compliance
Ingram Content Group UK Ltd.
Pitfield, Milton Keynes, MK11 3LW, UK
UKHW020816120325
456141UK00001B/98